Facebook® for Seniors

FACEBOOK® FOR SENIORS

CONNECT WITH FRIENDS AND FAMILY IN 12 EASY LESSONS

CARRIE EWIN, CHRIS EWIN, AND CHERYL EWIN

no starch
press

SAN FRANCISCO

Facebook® for Seniors. Copyright © 2017 by Carrie Ewin, Chris Ewin, and Cheryl Ewin.

Printed on demand in the U.S.A.

ISBN-10: 1-59327-791-1
ISBN-13: 978-1-59327-791-8

Publisher: William Pollock
Production Editor: Serena Yang
Cover Design: Beth Middleworth
Interior Design: Serena Yang
Developmental Editor: Liz Chadwick
Copyeditor: Barton D. Reed
Compositor: Serena Yang
Proofreader: James M. Fraleigh

For information on distribution, translations, or bulk sales, please contact No Starch Press, Inc. directly:

No Starch Press, Inc.
245 8th Street, San Francisco, CA 94103
phone: 1.415.863.9900; info@nostarch.com; www.nostarch.com

Library of Congress Cataloging-in-Publication Data

Names: Ewin, Carrie, author. | Ewin, Chris, author.
Title: Facebook for seniors : connect with friends and family in 12 easy
    lessons / by Carrie Ewin, Chris Ewin, and Cheryl Ewin.
Description: 1st Edition. | San Francisco : No Starch Press, [2017]
Identifiers: LCCN 2016036010 (print) | LCCN 2016051889 (ebook) | ISBN
    9781593277918 (pbk.) | ISBN 1593277911 (pbk.) | ISBN 9781593278090 (epub)
    | ISBN 1593278098 (epub) | ISBN 9781593278106 (mobi) | ISBN 1593278101
    (mobi)
Subjects: LCSH: Facebook (Electronic resource) | Computers and older people.
    | Internet and older people. | Online social networks. | Social media.
Classification: LCC HM743.F33 E95 2017 (print) | LCC HM743.F33 (ebook) | DDC
    004.084/6--dc23
LC record available at https://lccn.loc.gov/2016036010

Brief Contents

Contents in Detail

Acknowledgments

What a journey! There are so many people to thank for making this book possible. Starting at the beginning, we'd like to make special mention of Rojer Liberman for helping us fall in love with technology and giving us our beginnings with seniors. Lots of love to Kathy Rouse, Alex Taylor, Leslie Trevena, and Aldo Taranto for giving amazing presentations to seniors. Our sincerest thanks go straight to Lorna Stevenson for being a wonderful rock of support.

We're blessed with lovely family, and to each of you, we can only give our most profound thanks. We're also lucky to have incredibly supportive friends who've been behind us every step of the way, especially Elissa, Grace, Laura, Alex, Cat, Jinah, Alana, Kate, and Belinda. Your support has been amazing. We couldn't ask for better friends.

We must also thank the wonderful people at No Starch Press. From making excellent improvements, to incorporating our many changes (because one of us is a perfectionist!), to making things look amazing, and to being the best cheerleaders we could ask for, there's nothing you haven't been ready to do. Most especially, our passionate thanks to Bill, Liz, Serena, and Anna.

Of course, not a step of this journey would have been possible without the endless numbers of delightful seniors we've had the pleasure of teaching over the years at Seniors IT and the Chelsea PC Support Group. Thank you all!

INTRODUCTION

Welcome to *Facebook for Seniors*! Facebook provides a wonderful way to stay in contact with friends and family. Together you can enjoy sharing news, photos, games, private conversations, and invitations to events. You'll even enjoy the company of new people by chatting about topics that interest you in groups. Most excitingly, Facebook has never been more popular among seniors. Let's leap into the Facebook revolution!

This book will help you learn to use Facebook's most useful and beloved features in a really simple way. In no time at all, you'll learn to create an account, find friends, join topical discussion groups, play games, invite friends to important events, and share news, messages, and photos with family and friends.

About This Book

This book has been inspired by seniors just like you! We've been teaching for a combined 30 years and have had the pleasure of working with countless seniors in the classroom. We've loved teaching seniors so much that we've created a Seniors IT program dedicated to helping seniors learn how to use computers! Over the years, lots of seniors have asked us to turn our famous Seniors IT classes into a book so they can learn when and where they want with our simple style and activities. Well, here we are!

This book will help you discover the wonders of Facebook in the very same 12 lessons that we teach to seniors in our classrooms. This means that this book only covers truly useful Facebook features that other seniors have used and loved. This book helps you learn with step-by-step instructions and full-color pictures that you can follow along with on Facebook. No dry reading here! To help you perfect the skills you'll learn, we have lots of activities carefully placed in every lesson. This means you won't need to wait until the end of the lesson to try something.

Like many other seniors, you're probably worried about the risks of joining Facebook. Have no fear: we keep you safe by explaining what you should do to make sure your information is protected and your account is secure.

In summary, this book will help you learn the things you truly want to learn on Facebook! We hope you fall in love with Facebook and the wonderful connections it can bring with your friends and family.

WHO SHOULD READ THIS BOOK?

If you're a senior (regardless of whether you are at the younger or older end of the range!) and would like to share moments, memories, and fun with your friends and family on the internet, then you've picked the perfect book. It will be a big help if you've used a computer before and feel comfortable with basic skills like moving the mouse, using the internet, and typing.

WHAT YOU'LL NEED

Throughout this book, we assume that you have regular access to a computer and the internet and that you have an email address you can access. The step-by-step instructions in this book are based on Facebook's website rather than a Facebook App (such as you would download from the Windows Store or the Apple Store). You can reach Facebook's website from any device, so make sure that you follow along using the website rather than an app.

In this book we've also mostly assumed that you're using a Windows computer, although in key places instructions for an Apple computer are also included. If you're using a different device, such as an iPad or other tablet, you can still use this book and lots of things will be the same. Just be prepared for a couple of things to be different!

HOW TO READ THIS BOOK

We strongly recommend that you read this book in order because every lesson builds on the previous one. For example, it's very hard to add photos to your Facebook account before you've created a Facebook account!

Every lesson includes activities that put your learning into practice. Go and ahead and do all the activities! They have been designed to seamlessly fit into each lesson so you don't have to worry about losing your place. A couple of lessons and activities will ask you to work with a friend or family member to enjoy the full Facebook experience. If you can't find anyone to help you at a particular moment, feel free to leave the activity and come back to it later. To help make sure you're getting things right, the activities have hints or answers included in the back of the book. (See "Solutions" on page 285.)

WHAT'S IN THIS BOOK?

As you work your way through this book, you'll build your Facebook skills and knowledge. You'll start off by creating an account and learning your way around Facebook. Next, you'll build your own Profile and add friends to start your Facebook experience. After that, you can enjoy connecting with other Facebook users by posting messages and photos on your Profile and the Profiles of your friends and family. Then you'll dip into everything Facebook has to offer by playing games, joining topical groups, creating and responding to Events, and chatting in real time with friends and family. Lastly, we make sure you're safe and secure by looking at your privacy and security settings on Facebook. By the end of the book, you'll be confident and able to enjoy all of Facebook's key features. The lessons are laid out like so:

* **Lesson 1: Joining Facebook** introduces Facebook and helps you create an account.

* **Lesson 2: Meeting Facebook** provides an overview of Facebook's features and helps you learn your way around with confidence.

* **Lesson 3: Your Profile** introduces you to your personal page on Facebook to help you connect and share with your friends and family.

* **Lesson 4: Facebook Friends** helps you find and add Facebook friends and respond to friend requests from others.

* **Lesson 5: Creating Text Posts** helps you share exciting news, messages, ideas, and announcements with your friends and family through Facebook posts.

* **Lesson 6: Posting Photos and Videos** helps you share photos and videos with your friends and family through posts.

* **Lesson 7: Posting with Friends** helps you add written, photo, and video posts to the Profile pages of your friends and family.

* **Lesson 8: Playing Games** helps you find and play games by yourself and against your Facebook friends.

* **Lesson 9: Groups** helps you find and join a topical group and join in discussions.

* **Lesson 10: Messenger and Chat** helps you send messages and photos that only your friends and family can read and shows you how to chat with them live.

* **Lesson 11: Events** helps you create Event pages for real-life events you want your friends and family to attend, and respond to invitations sent to you.

* **Lesson 12: Privacy and Security** helps you feel safe on Facebook by showing you how to check and change your privacy and security settings.

What Else Do I Need to Know?

Although every effort has been made to make sure this book is as up to date as possible, Facebook is constantly improving, and you might find that small details have changed between the time this book was printed and when it reached your hands. For example, the screenshots might look slightly different from what you see onscreen or a button might have a different name or color. Regardless, you should still be able to identify what you need from the images provided.

Buckle in and enjoy your Facebook journey!

LESSON 1

JOINING FACEBOOK

Welcome to Facebook!
This lesson shows you how to sign up
for a Facebook account.

What Is Facebook?

Facebook is a *free* website designed to help you build and enjoy relationships with people. You might think of Facebook as a way to socialize online (for that reason, it's known as a *social network*). The idea of making friends and socializing online may sound strange at first, but as you've undoubtedly heard, Facebook is remarkably successful, with more than 1.5 billion users worldwide.

Essentially, once you've created your own Facebook account you can reach out and connect with existing friends and family, as well as new friends, who are also on Facebook. When you connect you can share exciting news, messages, ideas, photos, videos, live conversations in real time, event invitations, and games. Reaching out and asking to connect with a friend or family member on Facebook, or accepting their invitation to connect, is known as becoming Facebook friends.

WHAT CAN I DO WITH FACEBOOK?

Facebook provides an excellent way to stay in contact with friends and family, people who live far away, and old school friends from long ago. As a member of Facebook, you can do the following:

* Share exciting news about yourself

* Send private messages and have live, real-time conversations that only you and the recipient can read

* Share photos and videos

* Play Facebook games

* Join discussion groups to talk about common interests such as sewing, vintage cars, music, or sports

* Send and receive invitations to events such as birthday parties

Facebook is your door to a huge and thriving community of people where you can stay in touch, have fun, and participate in discussions, online games, and much more!

WHY CHOOSE FACEBOOK?

Facebook isn't the only website to offer so many social opportunities, but it's the largest by far, so there's an excellent chance that family members, friends, neighbors, and even long-lost school pals are already on Facebook. Estimates are that almost 30 percent of all seniors in America are using social networking sites like Facebook,[1] with more seniors signing up every day!

If you're worried about Facebook security and privacy, this book will help. Facebook takes privacy and security considerations very seriously, but there are particular steps you can take to make sure your personal information is even more secure and private. We'll examine the best ways to protect your privacy and security at every step, and Lesson 12 is entirely dedicated to fine-tuning your security settings so you have control.

Creating a Facebook Account

To begin your Facebook journey, you'll need to sign up for an account, also known as *joining* Facebook. This is a simple process, and we'll tackle every step. Once you've signed up, learning to use Facebook is pretty easy.

> **✳ NOTE:** *If you already have a Facebook account, just skip ahead to Lesson 2!*

To join Facebook you will need the following:

* Access to a computer and the internet

* An email address or mobile phone number

Once you've got everything ready, it's time to sign up.

---

1. Smith, Aaron, "Older Adults and Technology Use," Pew Research Center (April 3, 2014), *http://www.pewinternet.org/2014/04/03/older-adults-and-technology-use/.*

OPENING FACEBOOK

Facebook is a website, so you'll first need to open your internet browser. Different computers may have different browsers, like Microsoft Edge 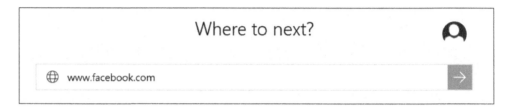, Internet Explorer , Google Chrome , Safari , or Mozilla Firefox , but any browser will work. You can also use Facebook as an app on a phone or tablet, but in this book we'll use the website. If you're using the Facebook app, switch over to the website now!

1   Enter the address for Facebook into your internet browser: *www.facebook.com*.

2   Press the ENTER key on your keyboard to load the Facebook website, shown here.

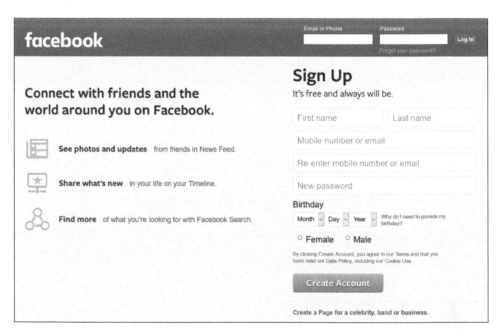

SIGNING UP

The Sign Up form appears on the main Facebook page. Depending on which internet browser you're using, this page may appear a little differently and you might see "Create an account" instead of "Sign up." However, the process will be exactly the same! Let's sign up for a Facebook account now.

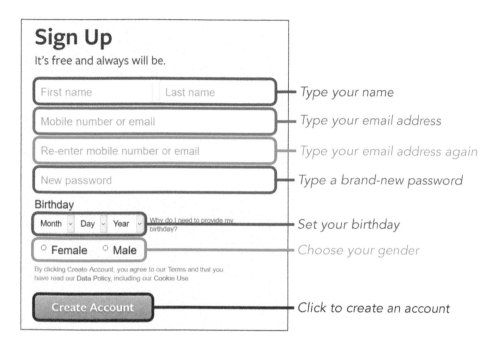

1. Click in the **First name** box and type in your first name. When you click in the box, the words displayed there will disappear and you can type in your details.

2. Click in the **Last name** box and enter your last name.

3. Click in the **Mobile number or email** box and type in one of these details.

    * NOTE: *You can join Facebook with an email address or a cell phone number, but email is probably safest. Facebook will use whatever you enter in this box to contact you, so be sure that you can access whichever option you choose.*

4   Enter your email address or cell phone number again in the **Re-enter mobile number or email** box. Make sure it is exactly the same as before.

5   Click in the **New password** box and enter a password. (See "Choosing a Strong Password" on the next page for tips.)

6   Enter your birthday. You can use your real birthday or a fake one—no one is checking! Click the arrows next to each of boxes to choose the day, month, and year of your birth from the lists that appear.

7   Choose your gender by clicking the round button next to either **Female** or **Male**.

8   Take a look at your form. It should look something like this:

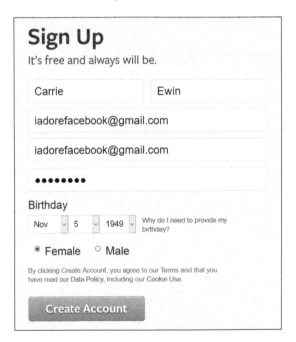

9   Once your form is complete, click the green **Create Account** button to complete your registration. (If you're using a different internet browser, your button may say something different, such as Sign Up.)

CHOOSING A STRONG PASSWORD

To keep your Facebook account safe, use a unique password, not one that you use for your email or anything else. Your password must be at least six characters long and should include numbers, letters, and punctuation marks. A secure password should not include factual information that others will know (like your name or birthday) or personal details that others can easily guess (like your pet or best friend's name). Also avoid well-known phrases or letters like *abc123* or *goodmorning*. An example of a good password would be something like *2dogs&1dragon*.

Once you've created a password, you can write it down— just be sure to keep it somewhere safe! If you're writing your password by hand, write carefully, and make sure that any capital letters, spaces, and punctuation marks are exactly as you typed them.

If you're comfortable with downloading and installing programs, you can use a password keeper program that creates secure passwords and then saves them for you; for example, LastPass (*www.lastpass.com*) or PassKeeper (*www.passkeeper.com*).

Skip Finding Friends

If you sign up using your email address, Facebook will prompt you to invite your email contacts to become your Facebook friends. To invite your email contacts as friends, Facebook needs access to your email contact address book. However, just as you would be wary of a store clerk asking for your address book, it's best to avoid offering Facebook more information than necessary. Also, some of the people in your email contacts are probably not personal friends you would wish to connect with on Facebook. For this reason, you can skip this step and add friends at a later time using a different method.

1 Click **Next** at the bottom of the "Find your friends" box.

2 Facebook will encourage you again to complete this step. Click **Skip Step**.

Congratulations, you've created your Facebook account! You'll now be taken to Facebook's Welcome page, which is shown on the next page. You have only a few more steps left to finish before your account will be set up!

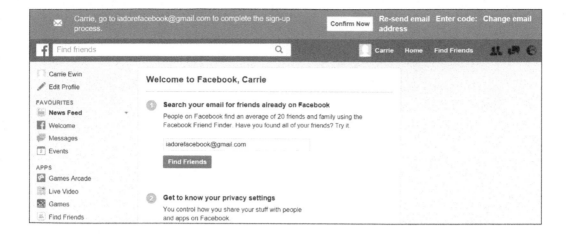

Confirm Your Email Address or Phone Number

Facebook next needs you to confirm that the email address or phone number you used to create your account really exists and that you can access it. This is to help make sure you're a real person. You will only be able to use your Facebook account for one day without completing the confirmation process.

1   Look at the top of the page for a message asking you to complete the signup process, as shown below.

2   Click **Confirm Now**.

3   You'll now be taken to your email account (or if you entered a cell number, you'll receive a text with a code that you'll now need to type in). You may need to sign in to your email account using your email address and password. Remember to sign in using your email account password rather than the password you just used to create your Facebook account!

4   If all goes well, Facebook should be able to confirm your account from this information, and you should see the comforting message shown below. Click **OK**.

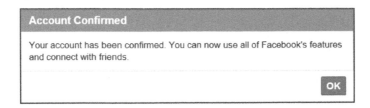

5   If you use a less popular email service, then Facebook may need more information. If so, open the email sent from Facebook. It will contain a confirmation code. The subject of the email will usually include the words "Confirm Your Facebook Account," similar to what's shown here.

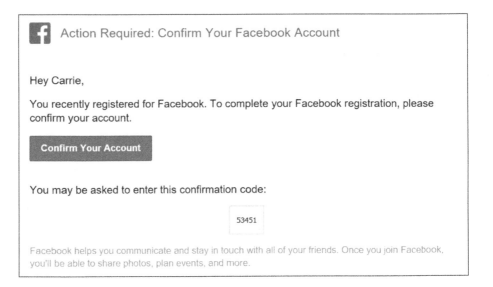

6   Click the **Confirm Your Account** button.

7   Facebook will load the same message shown in step 4 informing you that your account has been confirmed!

PROBLEMS SIGNING UP

Don't panic if you've come across a problem! Most problems in this process have simple fixes.

I Clicked Create Account but the Same Form Reappeared

If you didn't get past the Sign Up form, review the form to see if you missed something. If you did, the box with missing information should be highlighted in red and may have a red exclamation mark. Click in the box and enter the missing information. Then click **Create Account** again.

I See a Message Saying That My Email or Mobile Number Entries Don't Match

The Sign Up form requires you to enter your email address or mobile number twice. If these entries are not the same, you'll see an error message. Look over what you entered carefully, letter by letter or number by number, and correct the entry that's wrong. Then click **Create Account** again.

I See a Message Saying That My Email Address Is Invalid

This message usually means that your email address has been mistyped or that it isn't a real, working email address. Look closely at what you entered, especially the letters after the @ sign, and then re-enter your email address in the box. Then click **Create Account** again.

I See a Message Saying an Existing Account Is Associated with My Email Address

This message means that a Facebook account has already been created with this email address. This can happen if you previously joined Facebook and forgot that you used this email address. If you think you can remember your password, try to sign in to this account. If not, see "I Forgot My Password!" on page 25.

I See an Error Message About My Password

If you see an error message about your password, it means your password doesn't meet Facebook's minimum password requirements. Remember, your password must be at least six characters long and should include numbers, letters, and punctuation marks. If you see this message, click in the password box, delete the password, and type in a new one. Keep trying passwords until you come up with a strong one!

Adding a Profile Picture

Chances are good that you're not the only person on Facebook with your name. The world is a very big place after all, and 1.5 billion users make for a lot of overlapping names! For this reason you can add a picture next to your name to help identify you. This is known as a *Profile picture*. You can use any picture for your Profile that you like, even a picture of your favorite foods or animal—whatever you'd like your friends and family to see when they are trying to find you on Facebook.

Using your mouse, move down the Welcome page until you find the section titled "Upload a profile picture," shown on the next page. For your new Profile picture, you can use a picture already on your computer or you can use your computer's built-in camera (if it has one) to take a new picture.

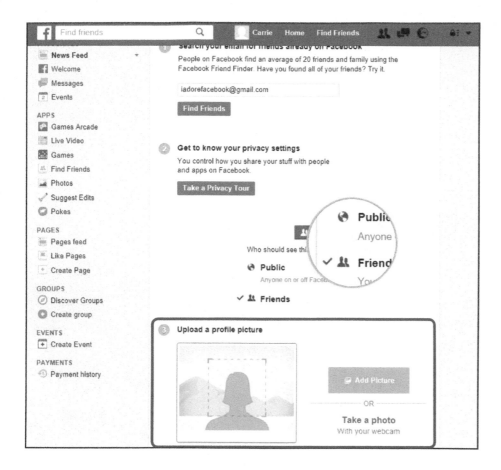

USING A PICTURE ALREADY ON YOUR COMPUTER

To add a picture you have on your computer, follow these instructions:

1   Click **Add Picture**, shown here.

2   You will now need to locate where on your computer the picture is stored. If you have a Windows computer, continue to the next section. If you have a Mac computer, skip to "Finding Pictures on a Mac Computer" on page 16.

Finding Pictures on a Windows Computer

To find pictures in the *Pictures* folder on a Windows computer, follow these instructions:

1   You can reach the *Pictures* folder using the File Explorer window that appears. Use the buttons on the left to locate *Pictures* and then click the folder to open it.

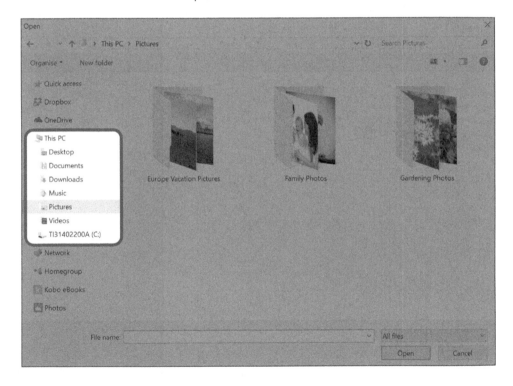

2   If you can't see *Pictures*, move your mouse over **This PC** and click the small arrow to the left. *Pictures* will now appear.

3 The image you want to add may be in the *Pictures* folder, or it might be inside another folder (for example, *Europe Vacation Pictures*). If it is, you can double-click (click the left mouse button twice in quick succession) the small image of the folder to open it and find your picture inside, as shown here.

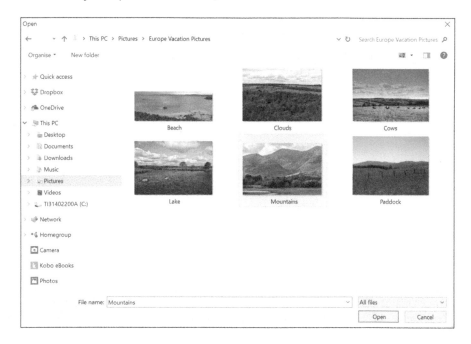

4 After you've found the picture, click it and then click **Open**.

5 Your picture will then become your new Profile picture!

Finding Pictures on a Mac Computer

To find pictures in the *Pictures* folder on a Mac computer, follow these instructions:

1   You can reach the *Pictures* folder using the File Explorer window that appears, as shown below. Use the buttons on the left to locate *Pictures* and then click the folder.

2   If you can't see *Pictures*, move your mouse over Favorites and click **show**. *Pictures* will now appear.

3   The image you want to add may be in the *Pictures* folder, or it might be inside another folder. If so, you can double-click (click the mouse button twice in quick succession) on the small image of the folder to open it and find your picture inside.

4   After you have located your picture, click the picture and then click **Choose** at the bottom of the *Pictures* folder, as shown next.

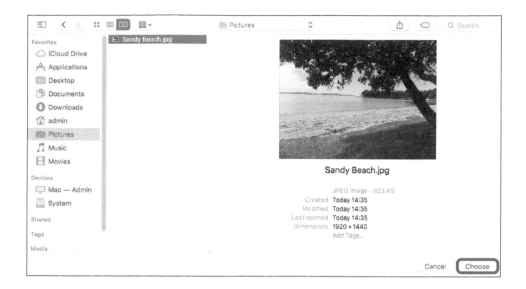

5 Your picture will then become your new Profile picture!

USING YOUR COMPUTER'S CAMERA

Many computers have small cameras (known as web cameras) either built in or perched on top. Using this camera, you can take a photo of yourself to create your Profile picture.

✱ **NOTE:** *If you click **Take a photo** and nothing happens, that means you don't have a web camera connected to your computer, and you'll have to take a photo another way and upload it to Facebook using the steps in the previous section.*

1   Make sure you're still on the Welcome page and looking at the section titled "Upload a profile picture."

2   Click **Take a photo**.

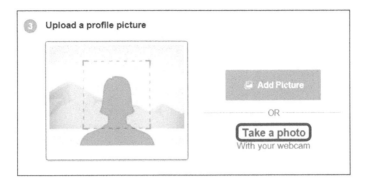

3   If you see a message indicating that Facebook would like permission to use your computer's camera, click **Yes**. Otherwise, you won't be able to take the photo.

4   Position yourself (or something else!) in front of the camera.

5   Click the **Take Photo** button. You should see a very brief countdown, so be sure to hold your position for a few moments!

6   Click **Save**.

7   This image will now become your Profile picture. You should know that your Profile picture is visible to anyone who visits Facebook, so make sure you're comfortable with what you put up there!

Congratulations! Your Facebook account has been created and confirmed. You are now a Facebook user, ready to enjoy all that Facebook has to offer.

Phew, We Did It!

Congratulations, you've completed Lesson 1! We examined:

*   Why seniors are falling in love with Facebook and why you should definitely do the same!

*   How to create a Facebook account and add a Profile picture

You're now ready to start using Facebook! In the next lesson you'll meet Facebook in much more detail.

LESSON 2

MEETING FACEBOOK

In this lesson, you'll meet Facebook and learn your way around so that you can dive into all that Facebook has to offer with confidence.

What Is Facebook For?

Now that you've created a Facebook account, you've become a bona fide Facebook user! Facebook has a lot to offer, so first let's look at what you might use Facebook for.

The main purpose of Facebook is to connect with other users. Facebook users you've connected with are known as *friends*, and your Facebook friends will usually be family members or friends who you already know or knew at some point in your life. After you've connected on Facebook, you can share and discuss your activities, news, life updates, stories, photos, and videos with each other. You can also play games together, chat live through typed messages, and send out invitations to events (like your birthday).

Oh Dear, Do I Need My Password?

To use the Facebook account that you created in the Introduction, you must be logged in. You're going to need the email address and password you created your Facebook account with, so before you begin this lesson, dig out your details!

LOGGING IN TO FACEBOOK

Follow these steps to log in to Facebook:

1   Open your internet browser. Whether the browser you use is Internet Explorer, Microsoft Edge, Safari, Google Chrome, or Mozilla Firefox, that won't make any difference to Facebook!

2   Enter **www.facebook.com** in the address bar, as shown below. The address bar is the long box at the top of the browser window that you can type website addresses into.

3 Press the ENTER key on your keyboard to load the Facebook website. You should see something like this:

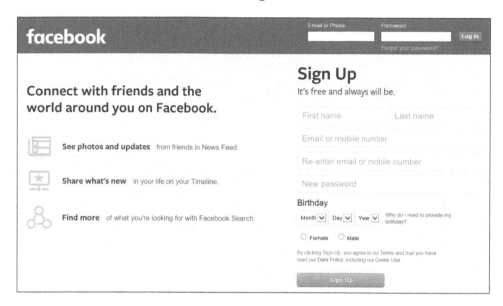

The blue bar at the top of the page is where you enter your email and password to log in.

4 Click in the **Email or Phone** box and then enter the email address you used when you created your Facebook account.

5 Now click in the **Password** box and enter your password, as shown below.

6 The password appears as dots to better protect your privacy. If you prefer to see your password text as you type, click the eye symbol at the end of the Password box (highlighted below).

7 Click the **Log In** button.

8 Congratulations! You should now be logged in to Facebook and should see a screen like this:

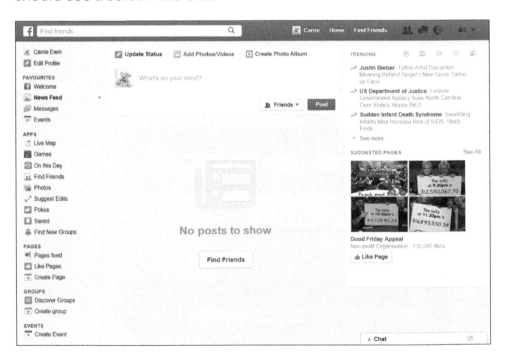

I FORGOT MY PASSWORD!

If you signed up for a Facebook account some time ago but you're not sure which email address or password you used to create your account, try signing in with the email and password you think you used. If that doesn't work, click the **Forgot your password?** option under the Password box, as shown here.

This will open a page where you can enter your name or email address to try to identify your account. If you can identify your account from the list Facebook provides, a new password will be emailed to you and you can log back in! If you can't rescue your previous account, you can sign up for a new one, but you'll have to use a completely different email address from the one you used for your existing account. This might mean that you need to create a brand-new email address as well.

LOGGING OUT OF FACEBOOK

If you share your computer with others or are using a public computer, always log out of Facebook once you're done using it. If you don't log out, others will be able to access your Facebook account.

1   To log out, find the blue strip at the top of the Facebook page.

2   Click the **downward-pointing arrow**.

3 Click **Log Out** in the menu that opens.

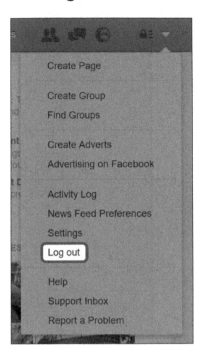

4 You should now be logged out of Facebook, as shown below.

ACTIVITY #1

In this activity, you're going to practice logging in and out of Facebook to keep your account safe.

1. If you've closed Facebook, open it again by typing **www.facebook.com** into your internet browser and pressing ENTER.

2. Log in to your Facebook account.

3. Try logging out of Facebook. Once you have successfully logged out, you should see the Facebook website displaying the Log In screen.

4. Log back in to your Facebook account.

Welcome to the News Feed Page

There's so much you can do on Facebook, but let's start by getting acquainted with the News Feed page. The News Feed page is Facebook's home page; it's the first page you'll see each time you log in to Facebook. It's a kind of mission control!

Log in to Facebook. If you've just created your account, you may see a Welcome screen instead of the News Feed page. If so, click the **News Feed** button from the left side of the page to open the News Feed page.

Let's explore the News Feed page now.

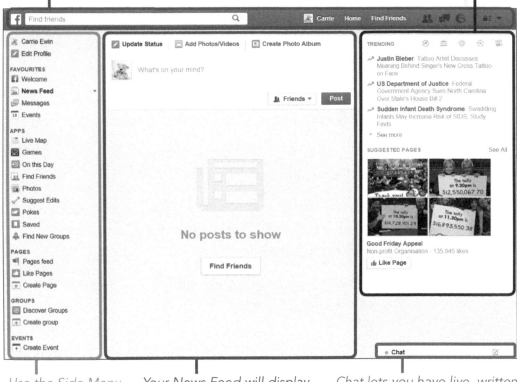

The Toolbar is a quick way to find things, reach useful pages, and get updates.

This section displays news stories, friend recommendations, or ads. Do your best to ignore the ads!

Use the Side Menu to go to pages on Facebook.

Your News Feed will display your friends' recent posts.

Chat lets you have live, written conversations with friends who are logged in to Facebook.

THE FACEBOOK TOOLBAR

The Facebook Toolbar will appear at the top of every Facebook page. It includes a number of buttons that give you quick ways of doing important jobs, like searching for friends and opening particular pages.

Let's take a look at each button, starting from the left. (All of these buttons and pages will be discussed in detail throughout this book.)

Return to the News Feed page

Open your profile page

Return to the News Feed page

Search for friends

Change your privacy settings

Search Facebook

See updates on friend requests, messages, profile posts, events, and games

Change your settings and get help

The f Button

Click this button to return to the News Feed page.

The Search Box

Use the search box to find the Profile pages of your Facebook friends, groups to join, and many other things. The description in your search box might change depending on which internet browser you're using. For example, your search box might read "Search Facebook" instead of "Find friends," but it won't make any difference to your search. You'll learn more about searching Facebook as you work through this book.

Your Name and Photo

This button shows your name and the picture you added when you set up your account. Click your name (*Carrie*, in this case) to move to your Profile page. Your Profile is your space on Facebook to share things like life updates and photos with your Facebook friends. We'll call this button the Profile button from now on. You'll learn more about your Profile in Lesson 3.

Home

Click this button to return to the News Feed page. (It does the same job as the Facebook f button!)

Find Friends

Click this button to search for other Facebook users. Once you find them, you can *request* to become their Facebook friend, which we'll look at in Lesson 4.

Friendship Notification

Click this button to see any updates about friend requests you have sent or requests that people have sent you. If this button has a red number next to it, you have new friend requests. Click the button to review them. You'll learn more about adding and accepting friends in Lesson 4.

Message Notification

Click this button to send a friend a message only the two of you can read (known as a *private message*) or to read private messages sent to you. If this button has a red number next to it, you have new messages. Click the button to view them. You'll learn more about private messages in Lesson 10.

Notification

Click this button to view notifications about activity on your Profile, such as if a friend posts a comment to your Profile or you've been invited to an event. If this button has a red number next to it, you have new notifications. Click the button to review them. You'll learn more about receiving notifications throughout this book!

Privacy Lock Icon

Click this button (which may look like a question mark, depending on your browser) to examine your privacy settings, which determine who can contact you and who can see the stories, photos, and videos you add to Facebook. You'll learn more about privacy throughout this book and in Lesson 12.

Downward-Pointing Arrow

Click this button to manage your account settings, including account security, seeking help, reporting a problem, and logging out of Facebook. We'll look at this in more detail in Lesson 12.

ACTIVITY #2

Try to answer these questions by choosing the correct button on the Facebook Toolbar.

1. If you wanted to review your Facebook privacy settings, which button would you click to begin?

2. If you wanted to find a dear friend to add her as a Facebook friend, which button might you click to begin?

3. If you wanted to see the latest photos added by your Facebook friend on her Profile, where would you enter her name to begin?

THE SIDE MENU

The Side Menu (circled at the top of the next page) provides a great way to access a lot of features. It appears only on the News Feed page, so to use it you need to open the News Feed page first. You'll get the hang of this very quickly and will find yourself using the News Feed page as your home base most of the time. The Side Menu will soon become your favorite way of moving around Facebook!

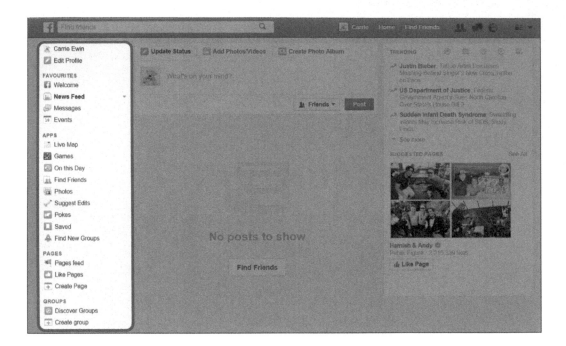

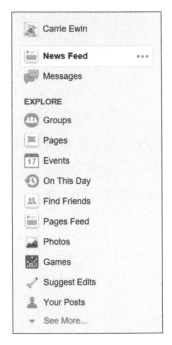

* NOTE: *If you created your Facebook account between 2015 and early 2016, and if you are using Facebook on Internet Explorer or Microsoft Edge, then your Side Menu may look a little different. Almost all of the same buttons will still be there, but your Side Menu may look like the image shown to the right.*

Let's explore some of the most important features that can be accessed from the Side Menu.

Your Name and Photo

Click your name (*Carrie Ewin*, in my case) to open your Profile page. This button does exactly the same job as clicking the Profile button (your name and photo) on the Facebook Toolbar at the top of the screen! You'll learn more about your Profile in Lesson 3.

Edit Profile

This button takes you to your biography, the section of your Profile where you can add or edit information about you.

Welcome

Click this button to read a short introduction to Facebook, which will appear in the News Feed column of the News Feed page. Your Welcome button will disappear after you've used Facebook a few times and might even already be gone from your Side Menu.

News Feed

The News Feed button takes you straight to the News Feed page! As you can see, Facebook gives you a lot of ways to return to the News Feed page, because it's the page you're likely to use most often. You'll learn more about the News Feed page in Lesson 7.

Messages

Use the Messages button to send a friend a private message or to read private messages sent to you. This button might also be called Messenger. You'll learn more about private messages in Lesson 10.

Events

Click the Events button to see notifications of upcoming Events. The Events feature helps you receive and send invitations to parties or gatherings. You'll learn more about the Events feature in Lesson 11.

Games

Use the Games button to find games to play. Facebook offers a huge selection of games that are free to play, like solitaire, blackjack, and chess. You can play against the computer or even against your Facebook friends! You'll learn more about Facebook games in Lesson 8.

Photos

Click the Photos button to quickly view photos you've added to Facebook.

Find Friends

Use the Find Friends button to search for people on Facebook and send them a friend request. This button does exactly the same job as the Find Friends button from the Facebook Toolbar, so you can click either button to begin finding friends. You'll learn more about finding friends in Lesson 4.

Discover Groups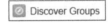

Click the Discover Groups button to find groups you might like to join. A Facebook Group can be like a club where people with similar interests come together to chat, such as a group dedicated to discussing gardening, or it can be used as a way to share information with a bunch of Facebook friends all at once—for instance, you might have a group with friends from the same high school. You'll learn more about Groups in Lesson 9.

THE NEWS FEED COLUMN

The News Feed column is the middle section of your News Feed page and is perhaps the main attraction of this page. The purpose of the News Feed column is to display stories, updates, news, photos, and videos from your Facebook friends. At the moment, before you've added any friends, your News Feed column will be empty, as shown on the next page.

But don't worry, because after you have added Facebook friends, your News Feed column will fill up with interesting posts, as shown below. Your News Feed column will then be an excellent place to get quick updates on what your Facebook friends have been doing. You'll learn more about the News Feed column in Lesson 7.

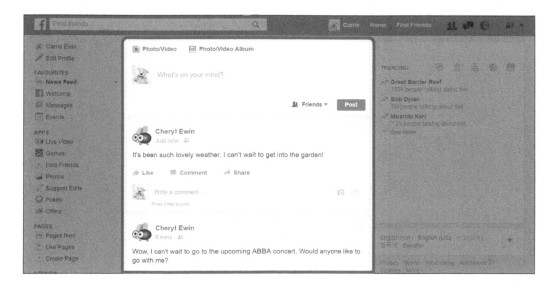

CHAT

The Chat feature lets you have instant, written conversations with Facebook friends. Chat conversations happen in real time, so as long as you and your friend are logged in to Facebook at the same time, you can be typing and reading conversations live! Using Chat invites your friend to respond right away, unlike a message or email, which might take a few days or more to get a response.

The Chat bar, shown below, is a small, rectangular box marked *Chat* that appears on every page of Facebook. When you click the Chat box, it will expand to show you a list of friends who are logged in and ready to chat. If your screen is larger, instead of this box you might see a column of names along the right side of your screen. You'll learn more about chatting in Lesson 10.

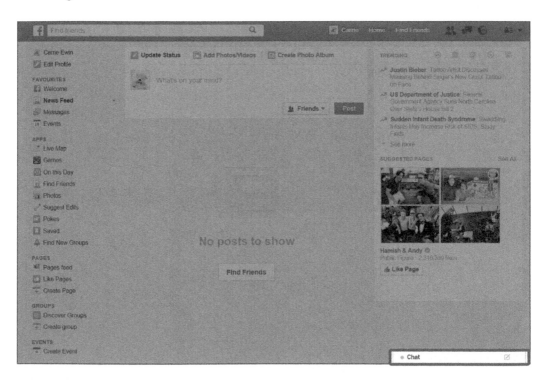

Phew, We Did It!

In this lesson, we covered some Facebook basics. We explored how to:

* Log in and out

* Recover a forgotten password

* Navigate the News Feed page

Now that you've met the many exciting features on Facebook, it's time to meet your Profile, which you'll do in the next lesson.

LESSON REVIEW

Congratulations, you've completed Lesson 2! Take this opportunity to review what you've learned by answering the following questions. If you can do so with confidence, you're ready for Lesson 3. If not, don't lose heart—just keep practicing!

1. How do you view your Profile page?

2. You would like to connect with an old buddy. Which button do you use to find him and add him as a friend?

3. If you want to play a new game, which button would you use to find it?

4. If you're concerned about your privacy settings, how do you review them?

LESSON 3
YOUR PROFILE

In this lesson, you'll meet the different parts of your Profile and learn how to update your Profile picture, cover photo, and biography.

Why Your Profile Is Useful

Your Profile is your personal page, where you can share details about yourself, updates on what you're doing, stories, and photos with all of your Facebook friends. Your friends will be able to see your Profile and use it to learn more about you and communicate with you. This means that your Profile should reflect who you are, what you're doing, and what you're interested in. Your Profile is useful for several things:

* **Telling other people on Facebook all about you:** If someone wants to find out more about you, they will most likely look at your Profile page—and if you want to find out more about someone else, you can look at theirs. Don't worry, you can control who can view your Profile page in your privacy settings. We'll cover that in the next section and in upcoming lessons.

* **Helping you share with friends and family:** Your friends and family can see the information and photos on your Profile page, and can respond with comments, photos, and videos of their own.

* **Connecting with friends and family:** Your Facebook friends can also add messages, photos, and videos to your Profile. You can comment on the items they add to open a conversation. By adding things to your Profile, you can connect and share with others!

Here are the kinds of things you might add to your Profile:

* Biographical information, like the name of your hometown or high school, places you've worked, and where you currently live

* Your interests and hobbies, such as your favorite sports team

* Small messages about your thoughts and experiences that your friends and family can read

* Photos and videos of anything you like

Just How Famous Will I Get?

In this lesson you'll add lots of personal information to your Profile. It's important to know who can see this information so that you know what to make available. Not everything you add should be shared with everyone! You can change the privacy settings of everything you add to your Profile, and you will learn how over the coming lessons. We also examine some more advanced privacy settings in Lesson 12.

In this lesson, though, you'll just get to know the default privacy settings. Here is what these default settings mean:

* Only you and your Facebook friends will be able to *add* or *see* a message, photo, or video on your Profile.

* The wider public will be able to see your name, your Profile picture, and your cover photo.

* When you add each item of biographical information (such as the name of your hometown), Facebook will ask you to choose who can see that piece of information. This could include your Facebook friends, anyone who visits your Profile page, or even just you. You learn how to add biographical information and choose the appropriate privacy setting in "Your Biography" on page 56.

You shouldn't be worried about adding personal information to Facebook, but you should be aware of what you're adding and who can see it. Over the coming lessons we explore this in much more detail and ensure that you have full control over who can see the information you add.

It's also important to add only the information you want to. Facebook will ask you a lot of questions, like where you went to school or what city you're from, but none of this is compulsory!

Getting to Your Profile Page

You can go to your Profile page like this:

1 Look toward the top of the Facebook page and find the blue strip, known as the *Facebook Toolbar*.

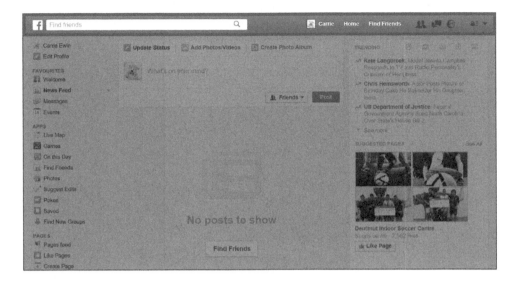

2 You should see your name with a little square photo, as circled in the image below. Click this button to open your Profile page.

3 You should now be taken to your Profile page. It should look a little bit like the figure on the next page.

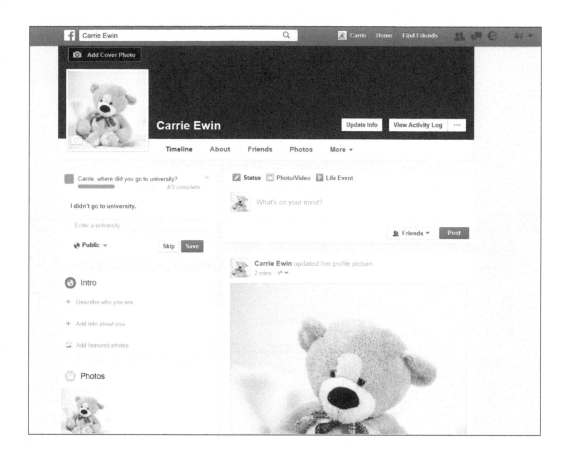

ACTIVITY #3

In this activity you'll be introduced to your own Profile page.
Try the following steps:

1. Open your Profile page.

2. Find where your name and Profile picture are displayed on
    the page.

Meeting Your Profile

A few different sections make up your Profile, so we'll begin by exploring the different parts. Later in this lesson, you'll learn how to build your Profile by adding biographical information. In Lessons 5 and 6, you'll learn how to put messages and pictures on your Profile.

The navigation pane shows your name, Profile picture, and cover photo. From here, you can also open other sections of your Profile.

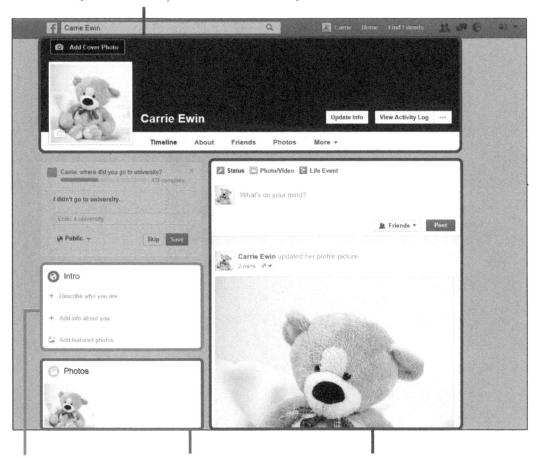

The Intro box shows your biographical information.

The Photos box shows photos you add.

The Timeline shows your Facebook activity and any messages or photos you and your friends add.

NAVIGATION PANE

The *navigation pane* at the top of your Profile page displays your name, Profile picture, cover photo, and the navigation buttons.

Your cover photo is a large photo that appears at the top of your Profile page.

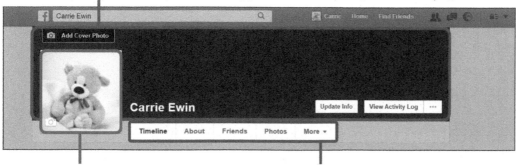

Your Profile picture is the image that represents you on Facebook.

These buttons take you to different parts of your Profile.

✳ Your *Profile picture* is the image you added when you first joined Facebook. This picture will represent you on Facebook and is always visible to the public, not just to your Facebook friends.

✳ Your *cover photo* is a larger image that you can upload like you did with your Profile picture. Because it's in landscape orientation, it gives you the opportunity to show off a particularly beautiful photo. This picture is also visible to the public, not just your Facebook friends.

✳ The navigation buttons take you to other sections of your Profile. Your Profile is bigger than it first appears! It includes the following sections.

The *Timeline* displays the messages, photos, and activities you and your Facebook friends have added. The *About* section displays all of your biographical information and any details you've added about your interests and hobbies. *Friends* is a list of your Facebook friends, and *Photos* shows a collection of all the photos you have added to your Profile. There's also a *More* section, which you should explore once you're more comfortable using your Profile.

INTRO BOX

The *Intro box* displays a small summary of your public biographical information. You haven't added any biographical information yet, but once you do, it will appear in this box if you've chosen to make the information viewable to the public. You can display your country or city of residence, the high school or college you attended, and other details. You'll learn to add this information, and control who can see it, in "Your Biography" on page 56. As you add your biographical details, the Intro box on your Profile will look something like this:

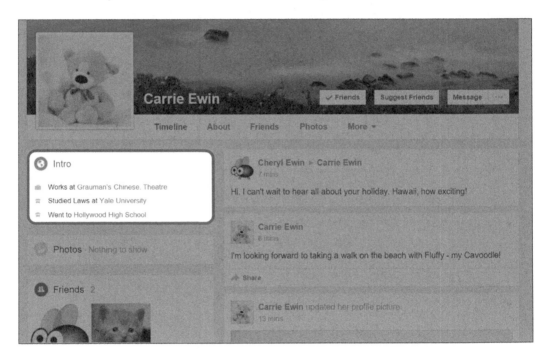

TIMELINE

The *Timeline* is the part of your Profile where you can add updates about your life, stories about your day, and photos and videos that you love. It is also where your Facebook friends can leave you messages as well as comment on your updates or photos. Your Timeline is your strongest link with your Facebook friends and can be your main method of communicating with them. As you and your Facebook friends add things to your Timeline, it will start filling up, as shown next.

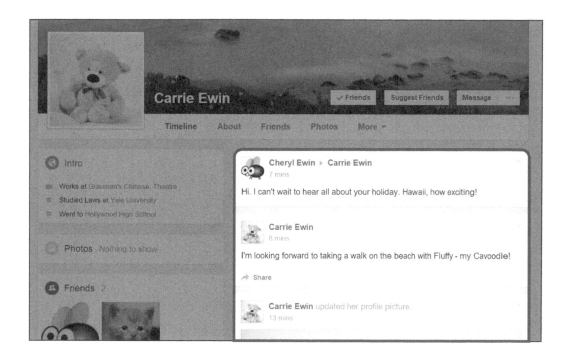

Your Timeline is organized by the date the stories or photos were added, so the newest stories will appear at the top.

ACTIVITY #4

Answer the following questions using your knowledge of your Profile:

1. If you want to read a story posted on your Profile by a friend, where on your Profile would you look?

2. If you would like to see the name of the city you live in, where on your Profile would you look?

3. If you want to see your Profile picture, where on your Profile would you look?

Your Profile Picture and Cover Photo

Your *Profile picture* is the image you added when you signed up on Facebook, and it represents you whenever you do anything on Facebook, appearing next to every message, photo, and video that you add. This helps other people recognize you and your contribution! Your *cover photo* is a larger image that's only displayed on your Profile page. These pictures are by default visible to anyone who goes on Facebook, not only your Facebook friends, so choose photos that you are comfortable sharing.

CHANGING YOUR PROFILE PICTURE

You can change your Profile picture at any time. This is useful if you want to add a new photo of yourself, or pictures of your pets, hobbies, favorite food, or just something you love. Changing your Profile picture is very similar to adding a Profile picture, which you did when you first created your Facebook account.

1   Click the **Profile button** to go to your Profile page.

2   Move your mouse over the top of your existing Profile picture.

3   Click the words **Update Profile Picture** that appear at the bottom of your Profile picture. You can either upload a picture that is already saved on your computer or take a new photo using your computer's web camera. You will have the option of taking a photo only if your computer has a web camera, though.

Uploading a Picture Saved on Your Computer

Follow these steps to upload a photo already saved on your computer:

1   Click **Upload Photo**, as shown next.

Update Profile Picture   ×

Upload Photo   Take Photo

2 This should open a File Explorer window. You now need to find where on your computer your picture is stored. Pictures are usually saved in the *Pictures* folder. Use the links on the left side of the window to find the *Pictures* folder and then click it.

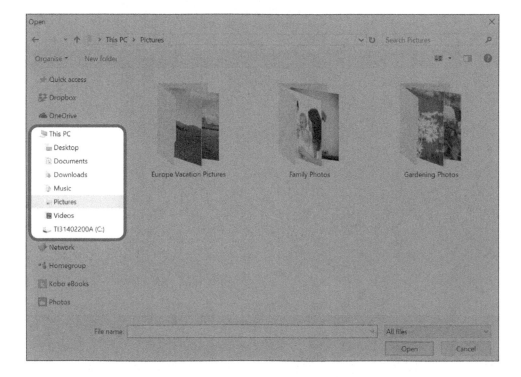

3 Find the picture you want to use as your Profile picture. Click it and then click the **Open** button located at the bottom of the window.

4 If your picture is big or a different shape than the Profile picture box, you may need to reposition the frame. Just click the picture and move it with your mouse. If your picture is too small or if you would like to zoom in on a particular part of the picture, use the slider at the bottom of the box and click and drag the circle toward the right. When you're happy with the position, click the **Save** button at the bottom of the box.

5 Your new Profile picture is now saved and you will be returned to your Profile. Notice your new Profile picture in the top-left corner.

Taking a Photo with Your Computer's Camera

To take a new photo using your computer's camera and upload it as your Profile picture, move your mouse over your existing Profile picture and click **Update Profile Picture**. Then, follow these steps:

1   Click **Take Photo**.

2   If you don't have a camera for your computer, nothing will happen when you click Take Photo. If you do have a camera, Facebook may request permission to use your web camera. If you want to take a photo from Facebook, you need to click **Yes** to allow this.

3   Your web camera will then switch on and you should see an image of yourself on your screen. Position yourself for your photo, and when you're ready, click the **Take Photo** button, as shown below.

4 Click **Save**.

5 Your new Profile picture is now saved and you will be returned to your Profile. Notice your new Profile picture in the top-left corner!

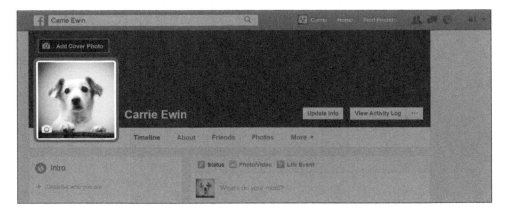

ACTIVITY #5

In this activity, you'll take a new Profile picture using your web camera. If your computer doesn't have a camera, you can skip this activity.

1. Think about the sort of Profile picture you want to represent you on Facebook. This could be a photo of you, or of something you love, a favorite food, a beautiful place, or a pet.

2. Arrange the picture you want in front of your computer's web camera. You could organize your grandchildren in a row, position your pet, arrange your favorite food on a plate, or even put a houseplant in the middle of the room!

3. Take a photo of the scene and update your Profile picture.

ADDING A COVER PHOTO

A cover photo is designed to give you more space to add a larger picture to your Profile. This image will only appear on your Profile page, and it can be anything you want. Often this is an ideal space to show off a picture of beautiful scenery. Remember, though, that the space available for your photo is long and rectangular, so try to choose an image that fits well in this space. Follow these steps to add a cover photo:

1 Go to your Profile page.

2 Click the **Add Cover Photo** button above your Profile picture.

3 You may see a box that tells you the purpose of a cover photo. Click **OK**.

4   You will then be presented with a small list of options for adding a cover photo. Click **Upload Photo**.

5   This should open a File Explorer window. Just like you did for the Profile picture, you will now need to locate where on the computer your pictures have been saved. Remember that pictures are usually saved in the *Pictures* folder.

6   When you've found a picture you'd like to have as your cover photo, click it and then click the **Open** button at the bottom of the window.

7   You'll be taken back to your Profile with the new cover photo in a suggested position. You can move the cover photo in the space by clicking it and dragging it with the mouse until your image is in a position you like. When you're happy, click **Save Changes** at the bottom of the cover photo, as shown below.

8 Your Profile will now reload with your new cover photo.

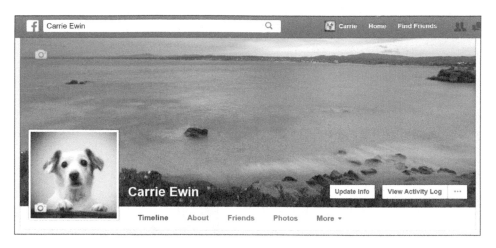

CHANGING YOUR COVER PHOTO

Changing your cover photo is very similar to adding a cover photo for the first time.

1 Click the small image of a camera in the top-left corner of your cover photo.

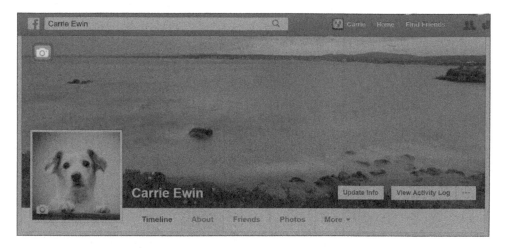

2 This opens the list of options, and you should see that there are a couple more options now, including Reposition and Remove.

If you just want to move your cover photo a little, click **Reposition** and use your mouse as you did earlier in step 7 of "Adding a Cover Photo" on page 54. If you want to delete your cover photo completely, click **Remove**, and you will be asked whether you are sure you want to remove the photo. Click **Confirm**.

3 To replace your cover photo with a new image, return to step 2 of "Adding a Cover Photo" on page 53 and continue with the steps until your cover photo has been changed.

Your Biography

Your biography page contains basic information about your life, such as where you're from, your workplace, and where you went to school. This can help your friends discover things they have in common with you. If you choose to assign a privacy setting of Public to some of your information, it can help your friends and family find the real you on Facebook as well. None of the information you can add here is required, so you can just add information you feel comfortable sharing with your Facebook friends and other users.

To open your biography page, follow these steps:

1 From the buttons below your name and cover photo, click **About**.

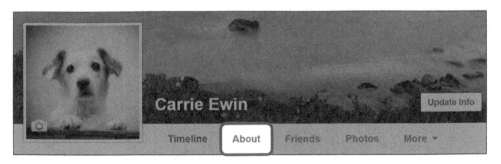

2 This will take you to your biography page. Categories are listed along the left side, while the most popular biographical details that people add are listed in the middle, as shown next.

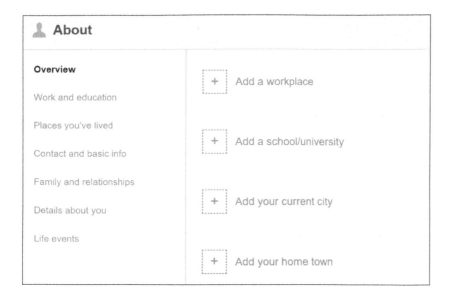

ADDING BIOGRAPHICAL INFORMATION

We'll only show you how to add your workplace to your biography here, but the steps to add other biographical details are very similar.

1 Click **Add a workplace**.

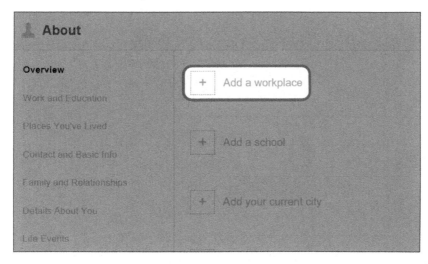

2 You will now be brought to the Work and Education section. Click **Add a workplace**, highlighted on the next page. (That's not a mistake—Add a workplace has to be clicked twice!)

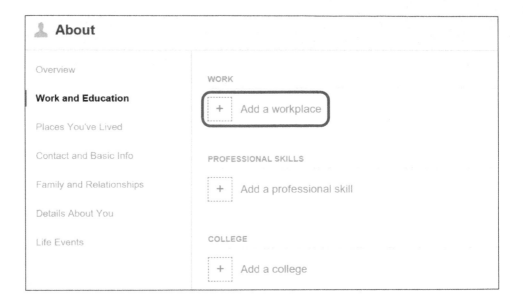

3 The Work form should now appear.

4 Click in each box and enter the information requested. As you type, you'll notice that Facebook tries to recognize many names and locations. Click the correct name from the list or click Create at the bottom of the list. Leave a box blank if you don't feel comfortable adding any particular piece of information!

5 If this is a past workplace, uncheck the **I currently work here** checkbox. Click **Add year** to choose the year you began, and click **Add year** again to choose the year you left.

6 When you've filled out all the details you want, click the **privacy icon** and choose who should see this information. You can choose Public if you'd like everyone to see it, Friends to let only your Facebook friends see it, or Only Me to make sure no one but you can see it. If you choose Public, the information will also appear in your Intro box!

7 Click the **Save Changes** button.

ACTIVITY #6

In this activity, try adding more information to your biography, such as the name of your high school or college!

EDITING AND CHANGING THE PRIVACY OF BIOGRAPHICAL INFORMATION

Your biography contains personal details you may prefer to keep private, such as your birthdate or where you work. Some of these details may also change from time to time. If you ever want to update a piece of biographical information or switch it to a different privacy setting, follow these steps:

1 From your biography page, choose the category of the piece of information you would like to change.

2 Find the piece of information you want to change, move your mouse over it, and hold it there for a few seconds.

3 Click the button that appears to the right of the information, as shown next. Depending on the information you're trying to change, this may be an Options or Edit button.

4 If you see an Options button, a menu will open. Click **Edit**.

5 The piece of information will then open for editing, as shown here.

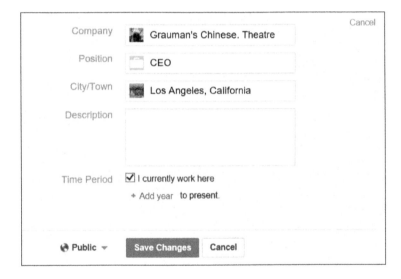

6 Click in the box that needs to be changed and enter the correct information.

7 If you would like to change the privacy of this information, click the **privacy button**, shown next.

8 From the small menu that appears, click **Friends** or **Only Me**.

9 Click **Save Changes**. Your biographical information will now be updated!

Phew, We Did It!

In this lesson you discovered the different features of your Facebook Profile page. Your Profile page is an important place to help others learn more about you and to connect with friends and family. Here's a recap of what you learned about:

* The purpose of a Profile page

* The information that your Profile page can contain, including biographical information; your written experiences, stories, and thoughts; your photos and videos; and the comments, photos, and videos added by your Facebook friends

* Who can see and add information to your Profile page

* How to open your Profile page

* The various parts of your Profile page

* How to change your Profile picture

* How to add and change your cover photo

* How to add biographical information

* How to edit and change the privacy settings of your biographical information

Fantastic work! In the next lesson you'll take the leap into finding and adding friends.

LESSON REVIEW

Congratulations, you've completed Lesson 3! Take this opportunity to review what you've learned by answering the following questions and completing the activities. If you can do so with confidence, you are ready for Lesson 4. If not, don't lose heart—just keep practicing!

Answer the following questions using your knowledge of your Profile:

1. You have just added a beautiful new cover picture. Where on your Profile page can your cover picture be found?

2. You would like to see a quick list of the photos that you have recently added to your Profile. Where on your Profile page can this list be found?

3. Your Facebook friend has written to you on your Profile telling you about getting a new puppy. Where on your Profile page would this new story be found?

Complete the following tasks:

1. Update your Profile picture by uploading a photo of your choosing.

2. Update your Profile picture again, but this time, select a photo that you've used as your Profile picture at least once before. This might be a bit tricky, as we didn't cover this exactly, but see if you can work it out!

LESSON 4
FACEBOOK FRIENDS

In this lesson you'll learn to
find and add Facebook friends.

Why Add Friends?

Facebook is all about connecting with friends and family, and to do this you need to add them as Facebook friends. A Facebook friend is a person you choose to connect with on Facebook. It can be anyone you know—from your closest relatives to far-flung school acquaintances. Adding a friend to Facebook means you can easily do the following:

* View their Profile, including their updates, stories, and experiences.

* View their biographical information, hobbies, and interests.

* Look at photos and videos they've added.

* Exchange messages, both privately and publicly.

* Play Facebook games together (like Solitaire).

* Send and receive invitations and responses to events (such as birthdays and parties).

* Share written conversations in real time.

Most importantly, when you add someone as a Facebook friend, you'll get updates about things they do on Facebook on your News Feed page and vice versa.

Friendship Privacy Settings

Becoming Facebook friends requires both you and the other person to agree to become friends. This helps ensure your safety on Facebook because you decide who can become your friend, and you have the power to reject invites from other users. Even if you have agreed to become friends with a person, you can always remove them, and they won't be notified that you've done this!

Your Facebook friends will be able to see everything on your Profile that you assign to a privacy setting of Friends. This will usually be your posted stories and messages, photos, hobbies and interests, and some of your biographical information. Remember, you can change the privacy setting of almost anything on Facebook, so you can also keep personal things away from the eyes of your friends! You'll learn more about privacy settings in every lesson and especially in Lesson 12.

Tips for Finding Friends on Facebook

You usually have the best chance of finding a friend by initially just searching using the person's name. But there are often lots of people with the same name on Facebook, so searching for a particular friend isn't always easy. If there are too many results or you can't find the person, here are some tips to help you find your friend:

* **Try adding more specific information about your friend.** You can search for friends using many different pieces of information, including their hometown, college, current city, or employer. Searching with multiple pieces of information can make it easier to identify the person you're looking for.

  Unfortunately, there is a limitation. This information will only help you find the person if they've added the information to their biography and set the privacy setting of the information to Public. For example, searching for Cheryl Ewin with a hometown of Melbourne, Victoria would only volunteer the Cheryl I am searching for if she has added Melbourne as her hometown in the biography of her Profile page and has also set the privacy setting on her hometown information to Public. Sometimes people don't add a lot of information to their biography, so trying to search using this information might not help you.

* **Modify your search information if you don't get the search results you're seeking.** For example, you may need to remove the hometown or college that you added to your search if the person you want doesn't appear in the search results.

✱ **Ask your friend what information they have added to their Facebook profile.** If you're already in contact with this person outside of Facebook, it can help to ask them what information they have included publicly in their biography. Knowing this will help you narrow your search accurately!

Finding a Friend

Facebook wants you to connect with people, so adding friends is quite simple. The first step is finding the friend you would like to add!

1 From the navigation bar at the top of the screen, click **Find Friends**.

2 If you scroll down the page, you'll see a Search for Friends form on the right. You'll use this to find friends. You might notice that the form has made searching suggestions using the information in your biography. This means that the form might look a little different to you.

3 Entering information in this form about the friend you're searching for will narrow your search. Remember, you can search for friends using any piece of information that you know about them, but it's usually best to begin your search with their name.

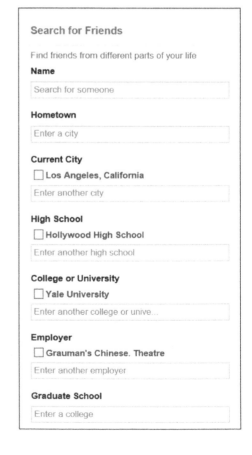

Search for Friends

Find friends from different parts of your life

Name

Search for someone

Hometown

Enter a city

Current City

☐ Los Angeles, California

Enter another city

High School

☐ Hollywood High School

Enter another high school

College or University

☐ Yale University

Enter another college or unive...

Employer

☐ Grauman's Chinese. Theatre

Enter another employer

Graduate School

Enter a college

4 In the Search for Friends form, click in the **Name** box.

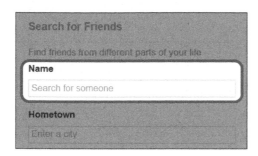

5 Type the name of the person you want to add as a friend. Facebook will try to recognize the name.

6 Click the correct name from the drop-down list that Facebook provides, as shown below, or finish typing out the name and press ENTER on your keyboard.

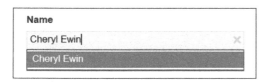

7 A list of Facebook users matching that name will appear.

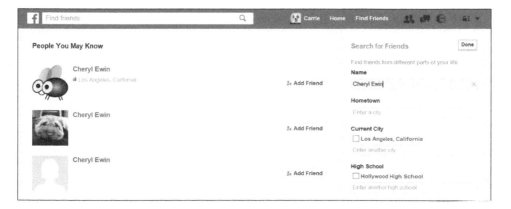

8 If you have a long list of results, continue to fill in the information in the search form to narrow the search.

9 Facebook will suggest search terms based on information you've added to your own Profile—for example, if you've listed your current city as Los Angeles, it will list that as a search option. This is designed to help you find friends that you're likely to know. To include this information in your search, simply check the box, as shown to the right.

10 A list of potential matches will appear. Now you can use a number of clues, including the following, to help work out which of the suggested people is actually the friend you are seeking:

* **Profile picture:** Most Facebook users will add a Profile picture—the small image that represents them on Facebook. Try and identify your friend by their Profile picture. Remember, not all of your friends will add Profile pictures of themselves. They could use a picture of a friend or family member, a hobby or interest, or even a pet!

* **Biographical information:** Look under the person's name to spot any publicly viewable biographical information that the search has found from the person's Profile. For example, in the following result, below Cheryl's name it lists that she works at Grauman's Chinese Theatre.

HELP! THE SEARCH HASN'T FOUND ANY RESULTS

If you add a search term (such as Current City) and Facebook tells you "No results found that match all of the following constraints," then your search hasn't found any results. It could be because your friend hasn't added that information in their Facebook Profile or hasn't made it public, or you may have made a mistake with that person's information. For example, you may have spelled their name incorrectly or forgotten what college they attended.

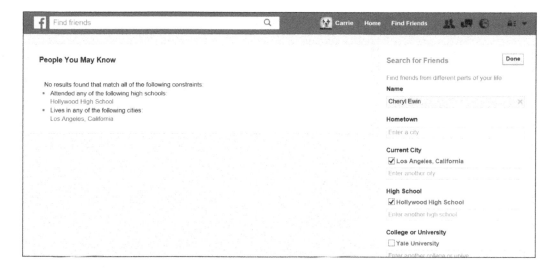

To continue searching, you'll need to remove the incorrect search information by clicking the checkbox next to the information, highlighted in the image to the right, to uncheck it. If you would like to remove the person's name, click the X to the right of the name.

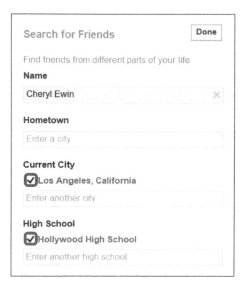

ACTIVITY #7

In this activity you're going to search for some people you know and would like to add as friends.

1. Search for a family member using only the Name box. Click the X next to the Name box to remove the name after the search.

2. Search using the Hometown box for a person you used to know. Click the X next to the Hometown box to remove the hometown after the search.

3. Search using the High School or College box for a person you went to school with. Click the X to remove the high school or college after the search.

4. Search for Cheryl Ewin, currently living in Los Angeles, who has a Hometown of Melbourne, Victoria.

CONFIRMING YOU'VE FOUND THE RIGHT PERSON

Now that you've found your friend, you should check that this is definitely the *right* friend! The easiest way to do this is to visit that person's Profile to guarantee their identity.

1   Click the person's name, written in blue.

2 This will take you to the person's Profile page.

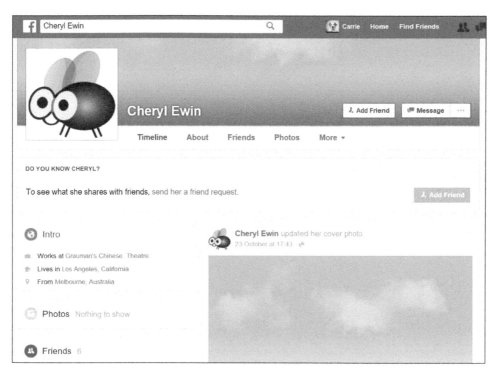

3 Remember that before you've connected as Facebook friends, you'll be viewing their Profile page as a member of the public, so you may not be able to see all of their information, depending on their privacy settings. Fortunately, you can use some further clues on their Profile page to confirm that this is the person you're seeking:

* **Cover photo:** Most people on Facebook add a cover photo. Find the cover photo just above the name and Profile picture and see if you recognize any people or locations.

* **About:** Click **About** to see the person's biography. If they've added biographical information, hobbies, or interests and set the privacy to Public, you'll be able to see this information. Make sure to scroll all the way down the About page, as some information might be at the bottom of the page.

* **Friends:** Click **Friends** to see a list of their Facebook friends. You may recognize some friends you have in common. If they've changed their privacy settings so that their friends list isn't visible to the public, you won't be able to see this list, and you will only be able to see any friends you have in common with this user.

* **Photos:** Click **Photos** to see any photos they've made available to the public. You may recognize the person or their friends and family in one of the photos.

ADDING A FRIEND

Once you're confident you've found the correct person, it's time to add them as a friend!

1 From their Profile, click **Add Friend**. (There are two Add Friend buttons—it doesn't matter which one you use!)

2 A friend request is instantaneously sent to this person!

ACTIVITY #8

In this activity, you'll find your new friend Carrie Ewin!

1. Use Find Friends to find your new friend, Carrie Ewin. Carrie lives in Los Angeles, California, studied at Yale, and her Profile picture looks like this:

2. Confirm that you've found the correct Carrie by looking for clues on Carrie's Profile. You know that Carrie loves this photo:

3. Click **Add Friend** to add Carrie as a friend.

RECEIVING AN ANSWER TO YOUR FRIEND REQUEST

The person will now be notified that you have sent a friend request. They will have the option of accepting or declining this request. If they accept the request, you'll get a notification.

1 A red number will appear on the friendship notification button in the navigation bar to indicate that you have a new notification.

2 Click the **friendship notification button**. The notification will tell you that this person has accepted your friend request. Congratulations, you're now friends!

3 Click the **friendship notification button** again to minimize the notification.

If your friend request is declined, you will not receive a notification.

Receiving Friend Requests

If your friends and family are already Facebook users, they may request *your* friendship before you get the chance to request *their* friendship. If so, it's up to you to accept or reject the request.

ACCEPTING OR REJECTING A FRIEND REQUEST

To accept or reject a friend request, follow these steps.

1 When you receive a friend request, a red number will appear on the friendship notification button to indicate that you have a new notification.

2   Click the **friendship notification button**.

3   You will see a request like the one shown below, including the person's Profile picture, name, and the option to accept or decline the friendship.

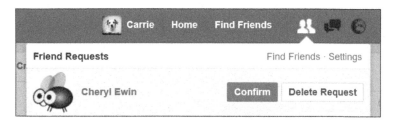

4   To accept and become friends, click **Confirm**.

5   To reject and not become friends, click **Delete Request**.

IF I REJECT A FRIEND REQUEST, WILL THEY BE TOLD?

No, the person won't be notified by Facebook that you have decided to reject them. Phew! However, they can check in the following ways:

* **By looking at your Profile:** Friends can see each other's Profiles. This means that friends can read all the messages, stories, experiences, photos, and biographical details that have been allocated the Friends privacy setting. If the rejected person visits your Profile and notices that they cannot see any of this information, no doubt they will realize you rejected their friend request.

* **By using View Sent Requests:** Savvy individuals may know that they can click **Find Friends** and then **View Sent Requests**. They can then view a list of all friend requests still awaiting an answer. If your name does not appear on the list and the two of you are not already Facebook friends, the person will know you rejected them.

Viewing the Profile Page of a Friend

The great advantage of adding a friend is that you can look at their Profile and enjoy the updates, stories, messages, photos, and videos that they've added! You'll learn much more about exploring a friend's Profile and leaving them written messages, updates, and photos in Lesson 7. But for now, let's have a quick look at how to visit your new friend's Profile.

1 From any page on Facebook, click in the search box.

2 Type the friend's name in the search box.

3 A list of Profiles matching your friend's name will appear, as shown below. Use the Profile picture that appears beside each name to help you determine which person is actually the friend you are seeking. Your friend will be one of the first Profiles in the list.

4 Click your friend's Profile from the list.

5 You will now arrive at your friend's Profile! Enjoy browsing their messages, updates, stories, and photos.

Now How Do I Remove a Friend?

If you decide you don't want to have a particular person as a Facebook friend anymore, Facebook allows you to remove the friend. This is more commonly known as *unfriending*. Usually you unfriend a person because you don't want them to be able to see the information or updates on your Profile anymore, perhaps because you've drifted out of contact.

REMOVING A FRIEND

To unfriend a user, follow these steps:

1   Go to your friend's Profile page.

2   Click the **Friends** button.

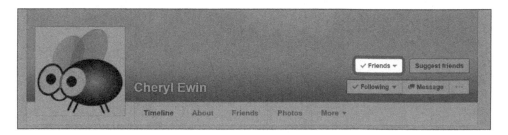

3   Click **Unfriend**.

4   The Profile page will then reload and you will no longer be friends. Fortunately, the unfriended user will not get a notification when you unfriend them!

ACTIVITY #9

In this activity you'll practice adding and removing a friend. Before you begin this activity, you might like to chat with your friend to explain that you'll be removing them and then adding them again!

1. Use **Find Friends** to add a friend or family member as a new Facebook friend.

2. Wait for them to accept you as a friend. Remember, you'll receive a notification when they've accepted you.

3. Remove your new friend.

4. Type the person's name in the search bar to open their Profile page and request their friendship again.

UNFOLLOWING A FRIEND

Perhaps some of your Facebook friends update too often, or the things they say are not to your taste, and you don't want to see these updates in your News Feed page every day. In these circumstances, if you don't want to remove that friend, you can choose to *unfollow* them instead, which means their updates won't appear in your News Feed page any longer. Importantly, you will still be friends, so you can continue to open their Profile page and read their updates or biographical information as you please. They will also still be able to see your Profile and any information with a privacy setting of Friends. Again, your friend will not be notified that you have done this!

1 Go to your friend's Profile page.

2 Click the **Following** button, as shown next.

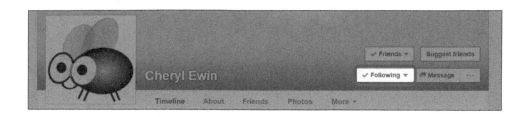

3   Click **Unfollow *Name of Friend*** (for example, *Unfollow Cheryl*).
    You will no longer see their posts in your News Feed page.

Phew, We Did It!

In this lesson you learned that adding friends unlocks Facebook's full
potential. This is the best way to share messages, experiences, thoughts,
photos, games, conversations, and much more. We learned how to:

*   Find friends using **Find Friends**

*   Confirm that you have indeed found the *right* person you would
    like to connect with

*   Add the friend

*   Accept or reject Facebook users that ask to be *your* friend

*   Remove or unfollow a friend

Congratulations on finding friends! In the next lesson, you'll learn to add
a written message or exciting piece of news to your Profile page as a post.

LESSON REVIEW

Congratulations, you've completed Lesson 4! Take this opportunity to review what you've learned by completing the following activities. If you can do so with confidence, you are ready for Lesson 5. If not, don't lose heart—just keep practicing!

1. Think of a friend or family member you'd like to add as a friend.

2. Open the **Find Friends** search feature and search for your new friend.

3. You can restrict your search results and increase your chances of finding the correct person quickly by entering more search information. Remember that this search information will only help find your friend if the information has been included in their biography and has been made publicly available.

4. When you think you've found the correct person, open their Profile page and then use the information available to confirm their identity.

5. Add this person as a friend.

6. Keep an eye on your notifications to find out when the person has accepted your friend request!

LESSON 5

CREATING TEXT POSTS

In this lesson, you'll learn to write life updates, stories, and experiences on your Profile page.

Why Post on My Own Profile?

A *post* is an entry you add to your Profile page that others can enjoy. Posts are often written text, but you can also post photos and videos. In this lesson, we'll look only at creating written posts, and then in the next lesson, you'll learn to post photos and videos.

It might help to think about posts like announcements you want to share with other people. This could be big news, such as "I'm retiring!" Or it could be something small you want to share, such as "The chocolate ice cream at Brown Dog Ice Cream is the best!" Posts you create on your Profile can (by default) be seen by your Facebook friends. If you'd like, you can change this privacy setting so that only you can see a post, or so the general public can see a post.

Many people join Facebook to enjoy news, photos, and conversations with family and friends, so it might seem a little baffling to post to your *own* Profile. But your Profile is not just for you to look at but also for your friends and, if you choose, the public to look at. By posting on your Facebook Profile, you're sharing your news with your friends and family and keeping them informed. Your posts may also appear on your friends' News Feed pages, and this is often how they will see your updates.

When your friends see your post, either on their News Feed or on your Profile, they have the option of replying or commenting on your post. This is one of the main features that make Facebook so enjoyable and exciting.

Creating a Post

Once you get the hang of posts, you'll find that they're quick and easy to create! You can create a post from either your Profile page or the News Feed page, and they'll both do almost the same thing. Creating a post from the News Feed page is a little quicker, which is excellent if you're in a hurry! However, if you use your Profile page to create a post, you'll see it appear on your Profile and you can make sure it looks perfect. Posting from your Profile also offers you a small number of extra options.

POSTING FROM YOUR PROFILE PAGE

Your Profile page offers an easy way to create a wonderful post your friends and family will love!

1 Click the **Profile button** to go to your Profile page.

2 Find the Post box at the top of your Timeline.

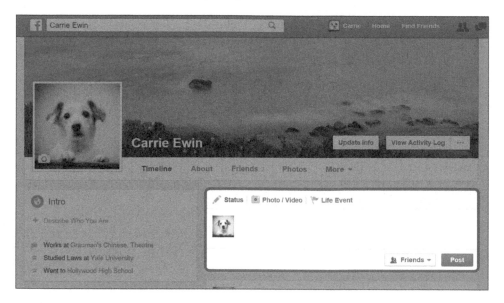

Notice that the box allows three different types of posts: Status, Photo/Video, and Life Event. The most common type of post is a Status post, where you write a message, experience, update, or funny joke. Essentially, you can write anything! If you want to add a photo or video, you would choose the second type of post (Photo/Video). The third type, Life Event, allows you to share the news of a very special life-changing event that happened on a particular date. In this lesson, we'll focus on Status posts.

3 The Status post option is enabled by default; it is marked by the small white arrow beneath the word *Status*, as shown below. If you clicked Photo/Video or Life Event, click Status to switch back.

4 Click in the box next to your Profile picture. You will then see the prompting words "What's on your mind?" These words will disappear when you start typing and won't be in your status.

5 Type out your post! It's very common for posts to be short and to the point, so it's good etiquette to keep your post fairly brief!

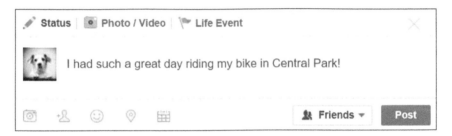

6 Click **Post**.

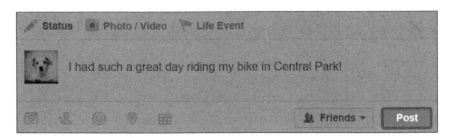

7 Your post has now been posted! It will appear on the Timeline section of your Profile page, as shown on the next page.

Let's take a closer look at your new post.

*Profile picture and name,
time of post, and privacy icon*   *Content of post*

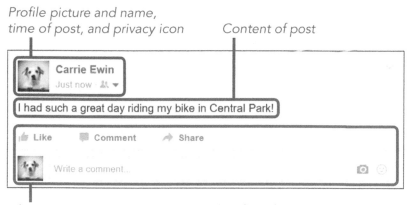

Like, comment, and share options that friends may use

✳ Your name and Profile picture will appear just above the post so your Facebook friends know who posted it.

✳ Just beneath your name it says when the post was made. Your post was made "Just now," so you know it's very recent.

* Next to the time, you'll notice the privacy icon (it looks like two silhouettes next to an arrow), which indicates who can see this post. By default, your post can be seen by your Facebook friends. We'll explore how to change this later in this lesson.

* Underneath the post, you'll see the options to like, comment, and share the post. Your Facebook friends can do these things to engage with you and your post! We'll explore most of these options later in this lesson.

ACTIVITY #10

In this activity, you're going to create a simple post.

1. Begin creating a post on your Profile about your day. You might want to say something quick and simple, like "What a lovely day!"

2. Click **Post** to post your message.

NAMING FRIENDS IN YOUR POST

You can name Facebook friends in your post to indicate that they were involved in your posted activity—or just because you particularly want them to see your post. This is known as *tagging* a friend. It can be a fun way of letting others know who shared your adventure or including your friends in your post.

When you tag a friend, the words "with *Name of Friend*" appear at the end of your post. The person you named will receive a notification encouraging them to look at the post and the post will appear on their Profile page and News Feed page. This means that their friends can also see the post.

1   Create a new post that says "I just enjoyed the most wonderful ice cream!" Don't post it yet!

2   At the bottom of your post, click the **tag icon**, highlighted below.

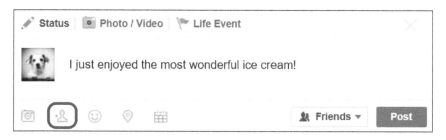

3   A box will appear underneath your post with the word "With" in it.

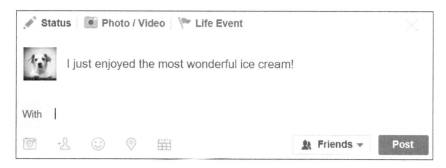

4   Click in the **With** box and start typing the name of one of your Facebook friends. As you type, you'll notice that Facebook recognizes the name. Click the correct friend from the list that Facebook provides.

5   Your post will now include the words "—with *Name of Friend.*" You can add more than one friend; just click next to your friend's name, type another name, and choose the correct friend from the drop-down list.

6   If you want to remove the tag from your post, click the small X just above their name in the With box.

7   Click **Post**! Your post will now appear as shown below.

ACTIVITY #11

In this activity, you're going to create a post and tag a friend.

1.   Begin creating a post on your Profile about a recent experience with a Facebook friend. For example, "Wow, I enjoyed dancing!" You can choose a different message to post.

2. Choose a Facebook friend to name or tag in your post. When you've chosen one, click the **tag icon** and tag your friend. Remember that you must choose a person who is already your Facebook friend. Your post will now read "Wow, I enjoyed dancing—with *Name of Friend.*"

3. Click **Post** to post your message with your friend tagged in it.

ADDING HOW YOU'RE FEELING

Sometimes written text just can't quite express your deepest feelings. You can illustrate your post by adding an icon of the emotion you want to associate with your post. (These icons are called *emoji* [pronounced *em-oh-gee*].) Adding an emoji is a good idea if your post is ambiguous or could be interpreted in a couple different ways. It also helps express the depth of your feelings to your friends and family.

1 Create a new post that says "Wow, the new Mamma Mia concert is just around the corner."

2 At the bottom of your post, click the **feeling icon**, highlighted below.

3 A long list of categories of feelings and actions will appear. Click **Feeling**, as shown next.

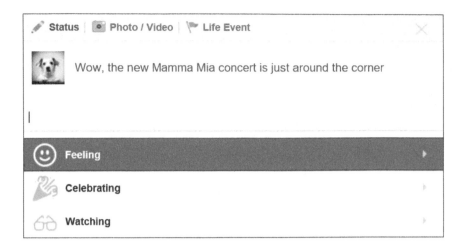

4   A long list of emotions will now appear, with a small illustration beside each one, as shown below. Move your mouse over the top of the list and scroll down to see more feelings!

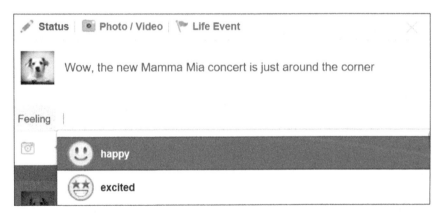

5   Click an emotion to add a "feeling" to the bottom of your post.

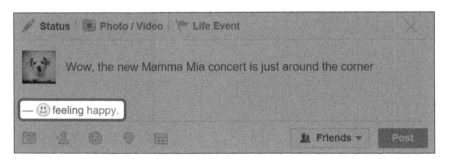

6 If you would like to remove the feeling emoji, click the X next to the feeling, highlighted below. If you can't see the box, click the **feeling icon** to bring up the Feeling box again.

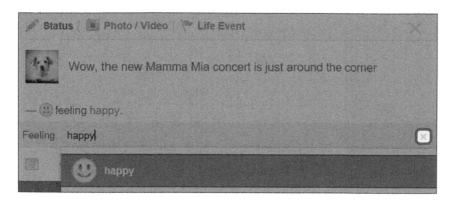

ADDING A LOCATION TO YOUR POST

You can also associate your post with a specific location. Our sample post has proclaimed that you're looking forward to the new *Mamma Mia* concert. However, your friends and family might not know where the next *Mamma Mia* concert will be, so it would be helpful to let them know that they can book their seat at Radio City Music Hall! Be aware, though, that many people don't like to give away their specific location. Rather than posting your location at a private home, for example, you may feel more comfortable adding a town or city as the location or choosing a public location nearby, such as a coffee shop.

1 At the bottom of your post, click the **location icon**, highlighted below.

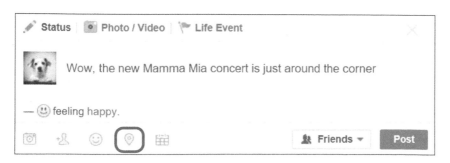

2   A Location box, starting with the word "At," will appear.

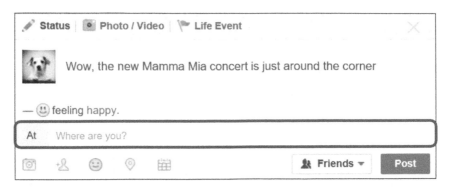

3   Click in the **At** box and type your location. As you type, you'll notice that Facebook tries to recognize the location. Click the correct location from the drop-down list that Facebook provides.

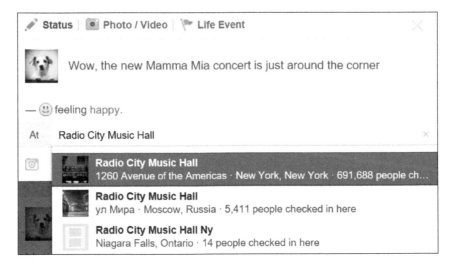

4   If you want to remove the location, just click the X next to the location, as highlighted on the next page. If you can't see the box with the location, click the **location icon** to bring up the box again.

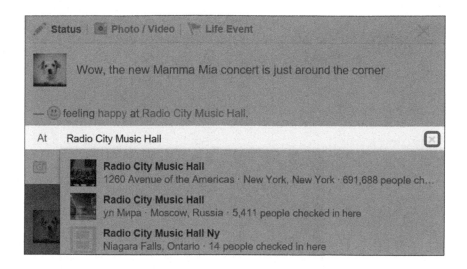

5 Your location will now be added to your post, and often with a handy map to make it even easier to visualize.

ACTIVITY #12

In this activity, you're going to create a post and add a location.

1. Begin creating a post on your Profile about a party or gathering. You might say something like, "I had a wonderful time at the book club."

2. Add the location of the event to your post. Remember, you don't have to be too specific. You could just add the town or city.

3. Post your message with the location added.

CHANGING PRIVACY SETTINGS FOR POSTS

By default, only your Facebook friends can read your posts. If you have named or tagged another person in your post, then by default that person's friends will also be able to read the post. However, you may prefer that some posts can be read by the general public and that others are kept more private. For this reason, you're able to change the privacy setting of each individual post.

If you are planning to make a post public, make sure you're careful about the information you put in it. You don't necessarily want to advertise that your house is empty while you're away, for example. If you wouldn't tell it to a stranger, then you shouldn't post the information publicly.

To change the privacy settings on a post, follow these steps.

1. Create a new post that says, "It's been a great day!"

2. At the bottom of the post you're creating, notice the privacy setting is set to Friends or, if you have tagged a friend, Friends (+).

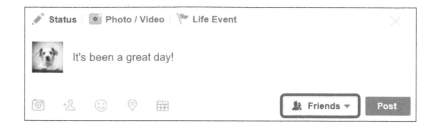

3   Click the **privacy button**, and a small menu will appear.

4   Click **More Options**.

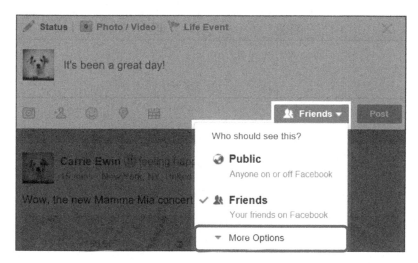

5   You'll now see the privacy options. If you choose **Public**, all Facebook users will be able to see this post. If you choose **Only Me**, only you and any friends you tagged will be able to see the information. If you choose **Custom**, you can decide exactly which friends you would like to be able to see the post and which friends should not be able to see the post.

6   Click the privacy setting you would like to apply to your post.

7   Click **Post**. Your post will now have your new privacy setting!

ACTIVITY #13

In this activity, we're going to create a post to share publicly.

1. Create a new post about the weather.

2. Change the privacy setting of the post to Public.

3. Click **Post** to share your message.

POSTING FROM THE NEWS FEED PAGE

You can also make posts from the News Feed page. This can be very handy because your News Feed page is the first page you see when you log in to Facebook, so you can just create your post right away. Posting from your News Feed page is very similar to posting from your Profile. A couple of very small options aren't available when posting from the News Feed page (such as changing the time and date of your post), but if you squint you won't notice any difference!

1 Click the **f** button to go to the News Feed page.

2 At the top of the page, you'll find the Post box. It looks like this:

3 Create your post using all the skills you've learned in this lesson!

Viewing Your Posts on Your Timeline

After you click **Post**, your post is sent to your Profile and to the News Feed of anyone who has the privacy permission to see it. All your posts remain on your Profile page. Here's how to see your old posts:

1   Click the **Profile button** to go to your Profile page.

2   All your posts appear in the Timeline section of your Profile page. Conveniently, they are all displayed in chronological order, so your newest posts will appear at the top of your page. Simply scroll down the page to see older posts.

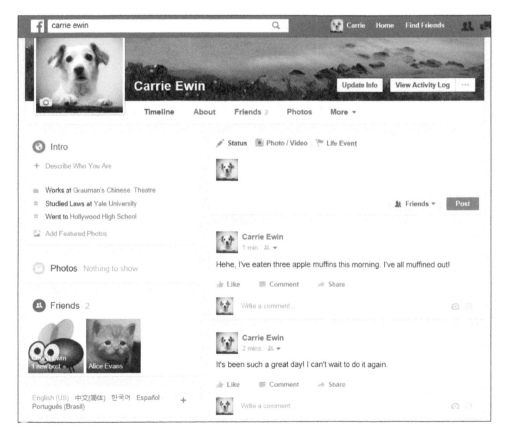

Receiving Likes, Reactions, and Comments

Your friends and family can respond to your post by *liking* it, which gives the post a thumbs up; by reacting to it, which gives the post a happy face, heart, or other emoji; and by commenting on it, which adds a written thought you can reply to.

RECEIVING LIKES ON YOUR POST

Liking is the Facebook version of a thumbs up, and you will get a small symbol of a thumbs up and the name of the person who liked your post at the bottom of your post. Just as it sounds, liking is quick way for people to let you know that they enjoyed a post! If your post has been liked, you will receive a notification.

1   A red number will appear on the notification button to indicate that you have a new notification.

2   Click the **notification button**. The notification will tell you that a friend has liked your post.

3   Click the notification to go to the post that has been liked.

4   Underneath the post, you'll notice the thumbs up symbol and the name of the friend or friends who have liked your post, as shown next.

RECEIVING REACTIONS ON YOUR POST

Your friends can also add a *reaction* to your post. A reaction works in exactly the same way as a Like, except that they can choose from a number of different reactions, including Love and Sad, with a different symbol for each. If you've received a reaction to your post, follow these steps:

1   A red number will appear on the notification button to indicate that you have a new notification.

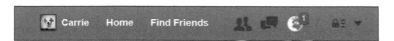

2   Click the **notification button**. The notification will tell you that a friend has reacted to your post, as shown below.

3   Click the notification to go to the post your friend has reacted to.

4   Underneath the post, notice the reaction symbol and the name of the friend or friends who have reacted to your post, as shown in the following figure. If you're not sure what the symbol means, you can move your mouse over the top of the symbol and hold it there for a few seconds, and the name of the reaction will appear.

RECEIVING COMMENTS ON YOUR POST

Your Facebook friends can share your experience by adding their thoughts about your life update, story, or experience. This is known as *commenting*, and allows your friends and family to essentially converse with you about your post. Receiving comments makes your news much more fun to share! Anyone who can see your post will also be able to see any attached comments from your Facebook friends. If someone has commented on your post, Facebook will send you a notification.

1   A red number will appear on the notification button to indicate that you have a new notification.

2   Click the **notification button**. The notification will tell you that a friend has commented on your post.

3   Click the notification to go to the post your friend commented on.

4   Your post will display, and you will find your friend's reply at the bottom of the post.

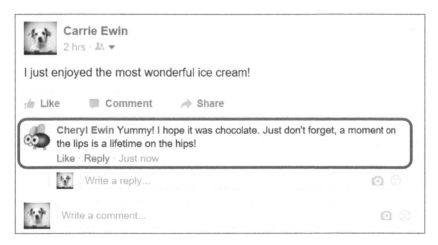

REPLYING TO COMMENTS ON YOUR POST

After your Facebook friends have commented on your post, you can continue the conversation by replying to their comments. If this sounds confusing, remember the following:

* You created the initial post: "I just enjoyed the most wonderful ice cream!"

* Your friend commented: "Yummy! I hope it was chocolate. Just don't forget, a moment on the lips is a lifetime on the hips!"

* You can reply to the comment: "Hehe but the ice cream is so worth it!"

By replying, you and your friend can really converse about your post. To reply to a comment, follow these steps:

1 Ensure that you are looking at your post with your friend's comment below it.

2 Find a box marked "Write a reply..." below your friend's comment.

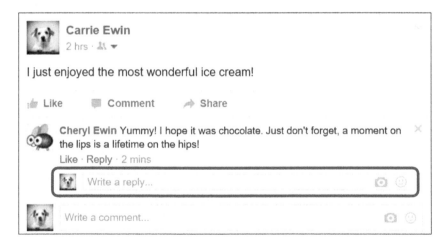

3 Click in the **Write a reply...** box directly underneath your friend's comment and then type your reply.

4 Press ENTER on your keyboard to send your reply.

5 Your reply will now appear underneath your friend's comment, as shown next. Your friend will receive a notification that you've replied to their comment.

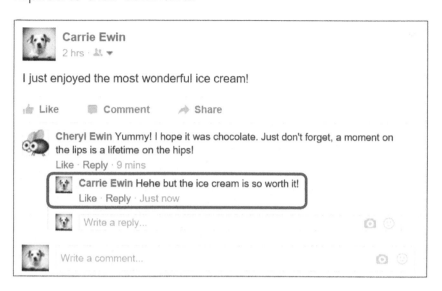

Deleting Posts

From embarrassing your dearest grandchild to potentially giving away information about a surprise party, there are many reasons you might wish to delete a post. Fortunately, no matter the reason, you can delete any post you've made at any time. If you delete a post, you'll also delete any comments your friends and family have written on the post.

1 Find the post you want to delete.

2 Click the small arrow in the top-right corner of the post, highlighted below.

3   A small menu will appear. Click **Delete**.

Save post

Edit Post

Change Date

Turn off notifications for this post

Hide from Timeline

Delete

Turn off translations

4   A box will appear asking you to confirm that you want to delete the post. Click **Delete Post**. The post will now be removed from your Profile.

Delete Post   ✕

This post will be deleted and you won't be able to find it anymore. You can also edit this post, if you just want to change something.

Cancel   Edit Post   Delete Post

Phew, We Did It!

In this lesson, we looked at posting on your own Profile. You learned that posts are exciting news, stories, and experiences you write about, or even photos or videos. In this lesson, we learned all about written posts. Here's what you learned to do in this lesson:

   ✳   Create a post from your Profile page and News Feed page

   ✳   Name or tag friends and family in posts

   ✳   Add a feeling or a location to a post

   ✳   Change the privacy setting of a post to Public or Only Me

* View likes, reactions, and comments on your posts

* Reply to a comment

* Delete a post

Great work! You've mastered text posts, so it's time to learn how to post photos and videos to your Profile page in the next lesson.

LESSON REVIEW

Congratulations, you've completed Lesson 5! Take this opportunity to review what you've learned by completing this activity. If you can do so with confidence, then you are ready for Lesson 6. If not, don't lose heart—keep practicing by creating posts and adding different details!

1. Create the following post on your Profile page: "I love this weather!"

2. Name or tag a friend or family member who also enjoys your current weather. (Lie if necessary; they'll forgive you!)

3. Add a feeling to show how you feel about the current weather.

4. Add your location so your friends and family know where the good weather is. Remember, this could be a large city or even a state; it doesn't have to be your very doorstep.

5. Carefully review the privacy setting of the current post and decide if it should be changed.

6. Post your post!

(continued)

7.	Remember to check your notification button to see if anyone has commented on your post.

8.	If there's a comment, reply to it.

LESSON 6
POSTING PHOTOS AND VIDEOS

In this lesson, you'll learn to spice up
your posts with photos and videos!

Working with Digital Photos

To post photos on Facebook, they must be in a digital format before they can be shared. Your photos should be in a digital format if:

* You took the photos with a digital camera.

* The photos were emailed to you and you saved the photo files to your computer.

* The photos were shot on film, developed, and then scanned into your computer.

* You found the photos on the internet and saved them to your computer.

ACTIVITY #14

In this activity, you're going to learn to save a picture from the internet to your computer. We're going to use a website called Public Domain Pictures. On this website, photo lovers have waived their rights under copyright law and have added their own pictures for anyone to use and enjoy freely.

1. Open your internet browser.

2. Enter *www.publicdomainpictures.net* into the address bar. Press the ENTER key on your keyboard to load the Public Domain Pictures website.

3. You'll see a collection of images on the home page. Scroll down until you find an image you like, or use the search bar at the top of the page to find a beautiful photo, and then click that image. It will then load in a larger size.

4. Right-click the image and a small menu like the one to the right will appear. From this menu, left-click **Save picture as**.

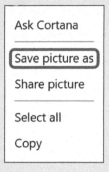

5. The File Explorer window will now appear. To be able to easily find it later, save this image to the *Pictures* folder. Click **Pictures** from the links on the left side of the menu, as shown below.

6. The text in the "File name" box should be highlighted blue, and you can just start typing a new name for your picture, as shown below. (If the text isn't blue, click in the box and delete what's there before you type a name.)

File name: | Durdle Door English Landscape

7. Click **Save**.

Congratulations, you now have a picture that can be posted on your Profile!

Posting Individual Photos and Videos

In the first part of this lesson, you'll learn to add photos to your Profile page one at a time. These photos will appear on your Profile as isolated pictures, something like a framed photo you might have around your house.

To keep things simple, we'll go through the instructions assuming you're adding a photo, but keep in mind that the same method can be used to add a video.

CHOOSING A PHOTO

Just like with written posts, you can post a photo from your Profile page or from your News Feed page. Using your Profile page helps you see all of your photos after they've been posted, so we'll use that method. Follow these steps:

1   Click the **Profile button** (the one with your name on it) to go to your Profile page.

2   Find the Post box at the top of your Timeline.

3   Click **Photo/Video**.

4 In the box that opens, click **Upload Photos/Videos**.

5 The File Explorer window will now open, and you'll need to locate where your pictures or videos have been saved on your computer. Pictures are often saved in the *Pictures* folder and videos are usually saved in the *Videos* folder. Look for *Pictures* or *Videos* on the left-hand side of the window, as shown to the right.

6 Once you've found your photo, click it and click the **Open** button.

7 Your photo should now appear in the bottom-left corner of your post, as shown here. Don't be concerned if it looks small; it won't be so small once it has been posted!

WRITING A MESSAGE TO ACCOMPANY A PHOTO

Your photo or video post can be improved by adding writing. For example, you can add text to your photo to discuss when and where it was taken or tell the story behind it.

1 Above the small image of your photo, note the words "Say something about this photo…" in the Post box, shown here.

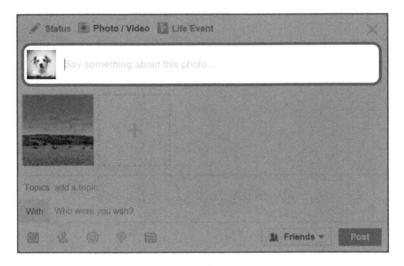

2 Click these words and type a message relating to your photo, like in the following example.

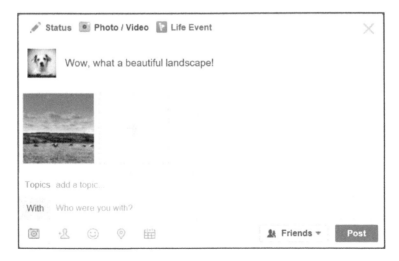

Be creative! Use all the techniques you learned in Lesson 5 to extend and improve your post. For example, you might want to:

* Click the **tag icon** to name a friend in the photo post.

* Click the **feeling icon** to describe the feeling you associate with the photo.

* Click the **location icon** to add where you took the photo.

CHANGING WHO CAN SEE YOUR PHOTO

As you learned in Lesson 5, the privacy of your post is set to Friends by default. This means that only your Facebook friends can see the post and the included photo. You can change the privacy setting of each individual post to allow the public or just yourself to view it. Before changing your privacy setting, think about who you want to see the photo; it's often a good idea to keep your photos fairly private.

1 At the bottom of your post, notice that the privacy button, highlighted next, is currently set to Friends.

2 Click the **privacy button** and a list of different privacy settings will appear, as shown below. Choosing **Public** means all Facebook users will be able to see the post, whereas choosing **Only Me** means no one but you will see the post.

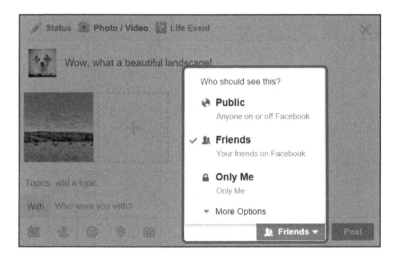

3 Choose a privacy setting.

POSTING YOUR PHOTO

The moment has finally arrived! You're now ready to post your photo.

1 Click **Post**.

2 Your post will now appear on your Profile page, like in the example here. Notice that your photo or video has appeared in full size! If you posted a video, it can now be played. You can play it by clicking the play button in the middle of the video.

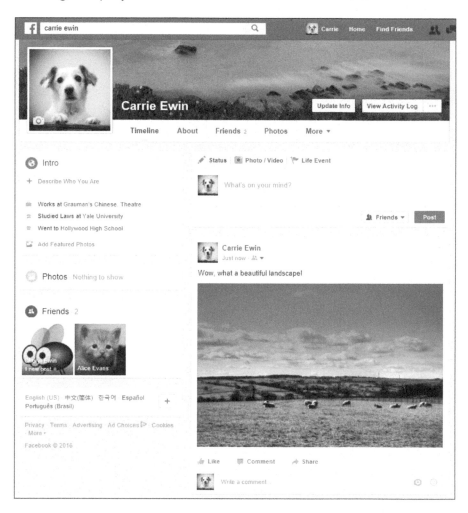

✻ NOTE: *You might be wondering why your photo hasn't appeared in the Photos box on your Profile page. Only tagged photos of you (that is, photos that are tagged with your name) appear there. To find other photos you've posted, click the Photos button from the navigation buttons under your name and Profile picture. All of your photos will be there!*

ACTIVITY #15

In this activity, you're going to add the picture you chose in Activity #14 to your Profile page.

1. Begin creating a new Photo/Video post on your Profile page and add the picture you found and saved from Public Domain Pictures.

2. Add a description just above the picture.

3. Leave the privacy setting of the picture as **Friends**.

4. Post the picture.

ACTIVITY #16

In this activity, you're going to take three photos and save them to your computer. You'll use these photos in Activity #17.

1. Using your digital camera, take three photos of beautiful flowers. If you don't have a digital camera, search for some pictures of flowers on the Public Domain Pictures website and save them to your computer (see Activity #14). You can use the search bar on the website to search for the term *flowers*, and you should be presented with lots of flower pictures to choose from!

2. Transfer the digital photos from your camera (or save the pictures from the website) to the *Pictures* folder.

Posting Photos and Videos in an Album

If you have a collection of similar photos or videos, perhaps from a particular vacation or event, you might want to group them together in an album. This will keep your photos organized and help your Facebook friends view the photos and videos they really want to see. Just as in the previous section, we'll show you how to add photos to keep things simple. But remember you can also add videos to albums!

CHOOSING THE PHOTOS

We'll create a photo album from your Profile page, but you can also do this from your News Feed page.

1 Click the **Profile button** (the one with your name on it) to go to your Profile page.

2 From the Post box, click the **Photo/Video** button like you did when posting an individual photo.

3 Click **Create Photo Album**, highlighted below.

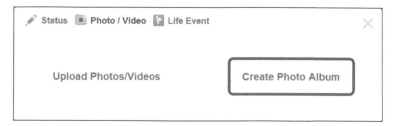

4 The File Explorer window will appear, showing the folders and files on your computer. Find the folder where you saved your pictures.

5 To select multiple photos, click the first photo, then hold down the CTRL key on your keyboard and click any additional photos you want to add.

6 When you've clicked all of the photos you want to use, let go of the CTRL key and click **Open**.

✶ NOTE: *If your photos are spread across a number of folders on your computer and you can't add them all at once, don't worry— you can add more photos from other folders later on. For now, just choose three photos to start the album off!*

CREATING THE ALBUM

The Create Album screen should now appear, with small versions of your chosen photos on the right and a Create Album panel on the left. Depending on which internet browser you're using, your album might be laid out a little differently, but the same buttons will exist!

Let's take a closer look at the Create Album panel.

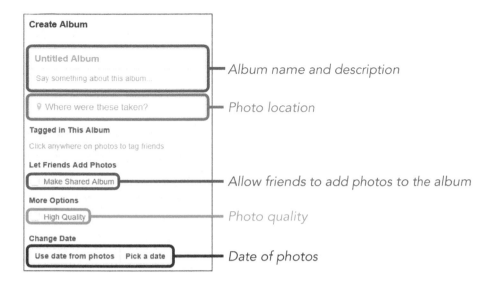

- Album name and description
- Photo location
- Allow friends to add photos to the album
- Photo quality
- Date of photos

*   Enter a name for your album in the **Untitled Album** box. You can also give a short description about your album in the **Say something about this album…** box. If you'd like to add a description to an individual photo, click in the **Say something about this photo…** box underneath it and enter a description. If you have a lot of photos, this can become overwhelming, so most people add only an album description.

*   Click in the **Where were these taken?** box and type in the location where the photos were taken. As you type, Facebook will try to recognize the location. Click the correct location from the drop-down list that Facebook provides. This will tag the location in each photo in the album.

*   To allow certain friends to add photos to your album, check the **Make Shared Album** box. Then click the **Add Contributors** box and enter the names of friends who can add photos to this album. Facebook will try to recognize their names; click the correct name from the drop-down list.

✱ NOTE: *Be a little wary, though—any friends you select can add any photo they like without your permission, and they can add additional contributors who could do the same!*

✱   If you would like your photos to display in higher quality, check the **High Quality** checkbox. This will make your photos look better, but they may take longer to appear.

✱   You can add a date to the album to let people know when the photos were taken. If the photos were taken with a digital camera that is set to the correct date, you can click **Use date from photos**. Otherwise you'll need to click **Pick a date**.

Click each of the three date boxes and choose the year, month, and day that the photos were taken from the menus that appear, as shown to the right. You can only choose  one date, so if the photos were taken on different days, just choose the most appropriate date for all of them. If you prefer, you can leave this blank and no date will be added.

ADDING AND REMOVING PHOTOS IN AN ALBUM

Sometimes after you've made an album, you'll realize that you forgot the best photo of all! But don't worry—additional photos can still be added.

1   From the Create Album box, click **Add More Photos/Videos**.

2 The File Explorer window will appear. Click the photo you want to add to your album. If you want to add more than one photo, hold down the CTRL key on your keyboard and click any additional photos.

3 When you've selected the photos you want to add, let go of the CTRL key and click **Open**. The additional photos will now appear in your Create Album box.

You can also remove a photo if you change your mind about including it. Simply move your mouse over the photo and click the X in the top-right corner of the photo.

CHANGING WHO CAN SEE THE ALBUM

The default privacy setting for your album is Friends, so only your friends and you can see your album. This can be changed to allow the public or just you to view the photos in the album. Be careful before changing this setting to Public, because your photos will then be visible to every person on Facebook!

✳ NOTE: *If you've allowed friends to add photos to your album, then by default these friends will also be able to see the album. You can also choose to let their friends view the album.*

1 At the bottom of your album, notice that the privacy button is currently set to Friends.

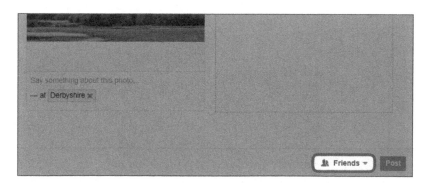

2 Click the **privacy button**.

3 Choose a privacy setting: Friends, Public, or Only Me.

POSTING THE ALBUM

The moment has finally arrived! Now you're ready to post the album.

1 Click **Post**.

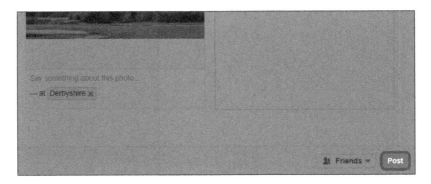

2 Congratulations, your album has now been created in the Photos section of your Profile page. You'll be automatically brought to your new album. It should look something like this:

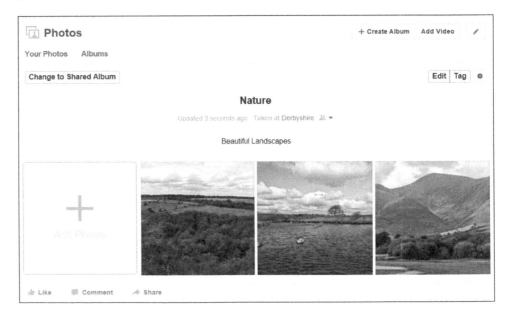

ACTIVITY #17

In this activity, you're going to create an album using the photos of the flowers you saved to your computer in Activity #16.

1. Create a new photo album post.

2. Add the three flower pictures into your album.

3. Add the title *Flowers*.

4. Add the description *A collection of flower photos*.

5. Add the location where you took the photos (or where they were likely taken).

6. Add the date that you took the photos (or today's date).

7. Ensure that the privacy setting of the album is set to Friends.

8. Post the album.

VIEWING PHOTOS IN AN ALBUM

After you've made your album, the photos in the album will be stored on your Profile so you and your Facebook friends can look back over these treasured memories at any time! Let's see how to view an album:

1   Click the **Profile button** (the one with your name on it) to go to your Profile page.

2   When you post a new album, it will appear on your Profile page as a post, as shown next.

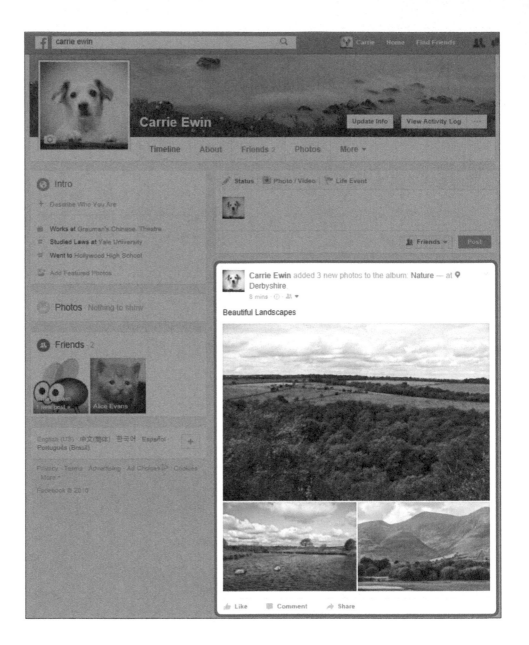

If you've added an album with a lot of photos, they may not all be visible in the post. The album will also show up on your friends' News Feed page if the album's privacy setting is either Friends or Public.

3 As you add more posts, your album will slip down the page and out of sight. To find the album and view all of the photos in it at any time, click **Photos** from the navigation buttons just under your name and cover photo.

4 Your photos will appear, with the most recent posts at the top. If you don't see the album you're looking for, click **Albums** from just above your photos. Find your album and click it.

5 Your album, and all of the photos inside the album, will then appear, but unfortunately they'll be quite small. To see a photo in full size, click the small version of the image (this is called the *thumbnail image*).

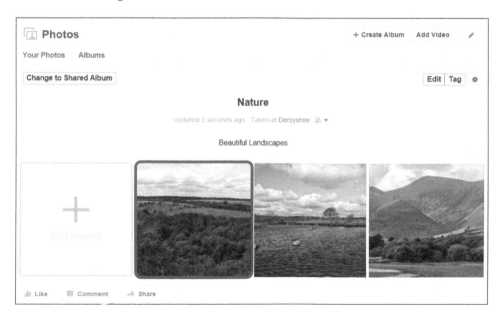

6 Your full-sized photo will appear!

7 Click the X in the top-right corner of the photo to return to your album.

ACTIVITY #18

Take a moment to view the beautiful flower photos you added to your album in Activity #17.

1. Find the photos by clicking **Photos** from the navigation buttons on your Profile and opening your album. (If your flowers album is the most recent album you've made, it will appear at the top. If not, look below to find your flowers album.)

2. Once you've found the photos, view them in full size.

3. Return to your Profile page.

Receiving Comments on Your Photos and Videos

Just like with written posts, your Facebook friends can share their thoughts about your photos and videos. This is known as *commenting*, and it's a wonderful way to share and receive feedback on your photos.

Your friends can comment on a particular photo or the entire album. Facebook will send you a notification when someone comments on a photo or album.

1 A red number will appear on the notification button to indicate that you have a new notification, as you've seen before.

2 Click the **notification button**, and the notification will tell you that someone has commented on a photo, video, or album.

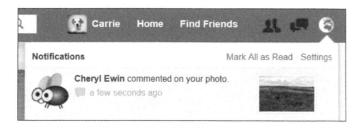

3 To view the comment, click this notification.

4 If the comment was received on an individual photo, that photo will display with the comment to the right of the image, as shown on the next page.

5 If the comment was received on an entire album, you'll be brought to the Photos section of your Profile with your album on display. You'll find the comment at the bottom of the album.

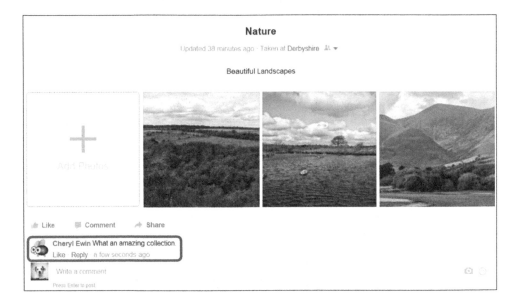

As with written posts, you can continue the conversation by replying to comments on your photos, videos, and albums. If you need a reminder on how to do this, turn back to "Replying to Comments on Your Post" on page 102.

ACTIVITY #19

In this activity, you'll check for comments on your album.

1. Check to see if you have a comment on your photo or album.

2. If you find a new comment, go ahead and read it.

Phew, We Did It!

In this lesson, we looked at posting photos and videos on your Profile. We extended these skills by choosing multiple photos with a similar theme and posting them together in an album. This helps keep photos and videos organized and encourages friends and family to enjoy viewing photos and videos of interest. In this lesson, you learned how to:

* Choose and post an individual photo

* Write a message to accompany the photo

* Create a photo album with a name, description, location, and date

* Add more photos to an album and remove photos from albums

* View the photos in an album

* Receive and reply to comments

Nice stuff! In the next lesson you'll build on these skills and learn to add written posts, photos, and videos to the Profile page of a friend.

LESSON REVIEW

Congratulations, you've completed Lesson 6! Take this opportunity to review what you've learned by completing the following activities. If you can do so with confidence, you're ready for Lesson 7. If not, don't lose heart—just keep practicing!

1. Start a new album on your Profile page with two of your favorite photos.

2. Add an album title, description, location, and date.

3. Add another photo to the album.

4. Post the album.

5. View the photos in the album at full size.

6. Return to your Profile page.

7. Remember to check the notification button for a comment on your photo, video, or album.

8. If there's a comment, reply to it!

LESSON 7

POSTING WITH FRIENDS

In this lesson, you'll learn how to post messages and photos on a friend's Profile, respond to posts, and view your News Feed.

Posting on a friend's Profile helps start up communication with your friends and family and is one of the most popular activities on Facebook! In this lesson, you'll also see what happens when a friend posts on your Profile, and you'll learn how to reply to keep the conversation flowing!

Visiting a Friend's Profile

Your Facebook friends have a Profile page just like yours, with biographical information, photos, and posts. You can visit the Profile of a Facebook friend to keep up to date with their happenings, learn new information, and share messages, photos, and videos. The News Feed page is also a great way to see what your friends have been doing, as a selection of their posts will appear on your News Feed. Remember, though, the News Feed page is only a snapshot of recent activity; if you want to learn more about a particular friend, it's best to visit their Profile page directly. Follow these steps to get to a friend's Profile page:

1   From any page on Facebook, click in the search box.

2   Type your friend's name in the search box.

3   A list of Profiles matching your friend's name will appear, as shown below. Use the Profile picture beside each name to determine which Profile belongs to the friend you're searching for.

4 Click your friend's Profile from the list. You will now arrive at your friend's Profile page! It should look something like this.

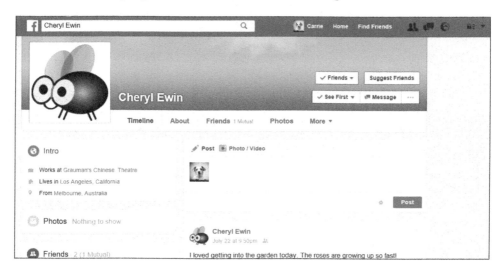

✱ **NOTE:** *If you're unsure which of the names on the list is the friend you're looking for, clicking a name and looking at the Profile is the quickest way to confirm! Use the tips from "Confirming You've Found the Right Person" on page 70 if you need further help.*

ACTIVITY #20

In this activity, you'll practice searching for and viewing friends' Profiles.

1. Type the name of a Facebook friend into the search box.

2. Click your friend's Profile from the resulting list to view this friend's Profile page.

3. Use the search box to find and open the Profile of a different friend that you can use for the next section of this lesson.

EXPLORING A FRIEND'S PROFILE

The good news is that every Profile has the same layout, so the Profile of a friend will be really similar to your own. This means you can quickly and easily find what you're interested in looking at! Let's take a quick look at your friend's Profile page, as labeled in the following figure.

The top section of a friend's Profile page displays their name as well as their cover and Profile pictures in a large format. The navigation buttons underneath allow you to view more information about your friend. Remember that you can do the following here:

* Click **About** to view all the biographical information about your friend and their interests and hobbies.

* Click **Friends** to view a list of all the friends your friend has added.

* Click **Photos** to view all your friend's photos.

* Click **More** to view your friend's interests and hobbies.

Intro Box

The Intro box displays some of the most important biographical details about your friend, such as their workplace, their current city, and their hometown. Just like on your own Profile, only information with a privacy setting of Public will be displayed in this summarized box. You can see more information by clicking **About** from the navigation buttons.

Photos Box

The Photos box shows a selection of your friend's photos. You can see all of your friend's photos by clicking **Photos** from the navigation buttons.

Friends Box

The Friends box displays a selection of your friend's friends. If you have any friends in common, they'll usually appear here.

Post Box

This is the box where you can post messages, photos, and videos on your friend's Profile.

Older Posts

This area shows posts that were previously added to your friend's Profile. These might be posts written by your friend or posts by other people. Just as *you* can post on your friend's Profile, so can their *other* friends!

RESPONDING TO POSTS

You can view all of your friend's posts in the Older Posts section of their Profile. You may also want to comment on, react to, or like their posts. We looked at this briefly in Lessons 5 and 6, when you received Likes, reactions, and comments from your friends. Now we'll look at how to like, react to, and comment on posts yourself.

To like or react to a post, follow these steps:

1 Find the post that you want to like, and click the **Like** button.

2 To add a reaction, hold your mouse over the Like button without clicking it. A range of reactions will pop up, as shown below, including Like, Love, Haha, Wow, Sad, and Angry.

3 Click a reaction and your reaction will appear just underneath your friend's post.

To comment on a post, do the following:

1 Find the post you want to comment on and locate the box marked "Write a comment..." at the bottom of the post.

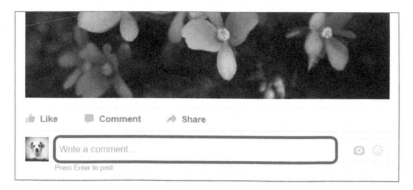

2 Click in this box and type your comment.

3 Press ENTER on your keyboard to send your message. Your comment will now appear underneath your friend's post.

SAVING PHOTOS FROM A POST

Your friend may post a photo (perhaps with you in it!) that you really like and want to keep. You can save it to your computer to view again later, send to family or friends, or even have it printed so you have a framed copy. To save your friend's photo to your computer, follow these steps:

1   Find the post with the photo you want to save.

2   Click the photo once to view it at its largest size, like so:

3   Right-click the photo and click **Save picture as**.

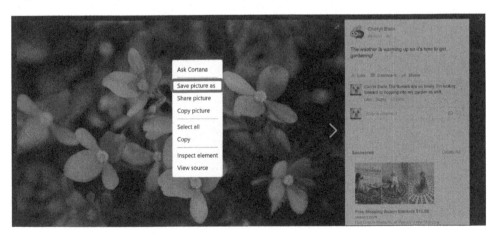

4   The File Explorer window will appear. Navigate to the folder where you want to save your picture.

5 Facebook will automatically give the file a long and obscure name, as shown below, but you can simply begin typing a new name to change this before you save it. Make sure you give it a name you'll remember later.

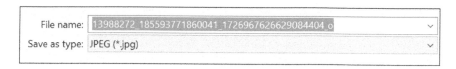

6 Click **Save** at the bottom of the File Explorer window.

Once you have the picture saved, you can print it or email it like you would any other file!

Posting on a Friend's Profile

The time has come! Let's look at how to add posts to your friend's Profile. Here are some things you might want to post:

* **Written messages:** You might want to say hello, catch up with your friend, or post a "Happy Birthday!" message. Facebook posts can also be used to make plans ("Would you be interested in seeing that new movie soon?") or discuss something you did together, such as attending a party or event.

* **Photos and videos:** You may want to post photos or videos on a friend's Profile to talk about events you both attended, to show off some vacation pictures, or to share your grandchild's first steps.

It's important to know that your friend has control over who can see the post on their Profile, even if you wrote it. So post carefully! Be aware that anyone might see your posts, so you shouldn't post anything too personal to a friend's Profile. If you would like to have a personal conversation, then private messages are the ideal way to do this. You'll learn all about private messages in Lesson 10!

POSTING WRITTEN MESSAGES

Let's first look at posting written messages to a friend's Profile.

1 Go to your friend's Profile page and find the Post box.

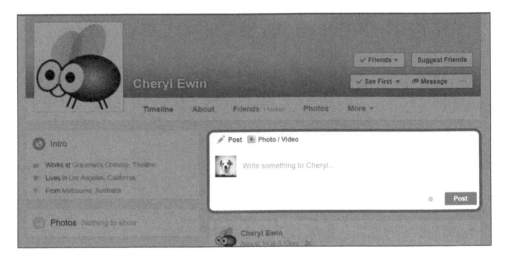

2 Click in the box next to your Profile picture and then type your message. It's often a good idea to keep it short and sweet.

3 When you're happy with your message, click **Post**. Your message will be posted on your friend's Profile!

ACTIVITY #21

Choose a Facebook friend you want to post a message to and then follow these steps:

1. Find your friend using the search box and visit their Profile.

2. Type a message in the Post box. If you can't think of anything to write, simply post a greeting such as "Howdy! How are you?"

3. Click **Post** to post your new message.

POSTING PHOTOS AND VIDEOS

By posting photos or videos on your friend's Profile, you can be sure that your friend sees those memories and moments. On a friend's Profile page, photos can only be posted individually, not as an album. Follow these steps to post a photo:

1 Go to your friend's Profile page and find the Post box. At the top of the box, click **Photo/Video**.

2 The box will then expand. Click the dashed square toward the bottom of the box, highlighted on the next page.

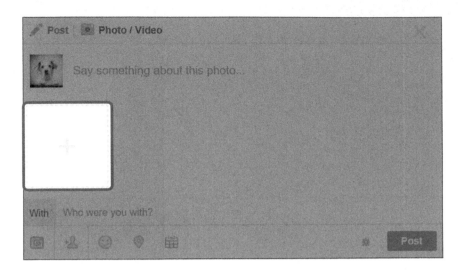

3 The File Explorer window will appear. Find where your photo is saved on your computer.

4 After you've located your photo (or video), click it and then click **Open**.

5 Your photo (or video) should now appear in the bottom-left corner of your post. Don't be concerned if it looks small. It won't actually appear so small after it has been posted!

6 Note the words "Say something about this photo..." above the small image of your photo. Click these words and then type a message to leave with the photo. When you're happy with your post, click **Post**.

ACTIVITY #22

Choose a Facebook friend whose Profile you would like to post on and then follow these steps:

1. Go to your friend's Profile page.

2. Choose a photo to post on your friend's Profile page. Once the photo has been added, write something about it.

3. Post your photo and message.

Receiving Posts from Friends

In the same way that you can post on a friend's Profile, they can post on yours! In this section, you'll learn how to view and comment on posts that your friends add to your Profile.

The prospect of other people posting on your Profile can be a little worrying! But don't be concerned: you have control over the privacy of everything on your Profile, even posts other people have written. The following are the default settings for your Profile:

⁕ Only your Facebook friends can post on your Profile. This includes written messages, photos, and videos.

⁕ Only your Facebook friends can see what others have posted on your Profile.

You can change these default settings if you want to, and we'll look at how to do that in Lesson 12.

VIEWING POSTS ON YOUR PROFILE

If a friend posts on your Profile, Facebook will send you a notification.

1 Locate the notification button on the Facebook Toolbar. A red number will appear on the notification button to indicate that you have a new notification.

2 Click the **notification button**. The notification will state that a friend has posted on your Timeline, as shown on the next page (remember, your Timeline is the section of your Profile where your posts appear).

3 Click this notification, and you will be taken to the post.

You can also view a friend's older post on your Profile at any time.

1 Click the **Profile button** to go to your Profile.

2 Scroll down through older posts to find a post you'd like to read.

RESPONDING TO POSTS ON YOUR PROFILE

Of course it's important to keep the conversation going! Just as you commented on your friend's posts on their own Profile page earlier in the lesson, you can comment on posts that your friends leave on your Profile.

1 View the post your friend added to your Profile.

2 At the bottom of the post, click in the **Write a comment...** box, as shown on the next page.

Cheryl Ewin ▶ Carrie Ewin
11 mins · 🐾

I knew you would love to see this gorgeous dog!

👍 Like   💬 Comment   ➤ Share

Write a comment...

3   Use the skills you learned in "Responding to Posts" on page 135 to like, react, and reply to your friend's post.

SPICING UP YOUR COMMENTS WITH STICKERS

Stickers are a great feature that only appear when you comment on a post, and not when you create a new post. You can add a sticker to a friend's post on their own Profile as well as a post on yours. These cute little stickers make a comment more interesting and expressive. There are dozens available, so you can find one to suit pretty much any situation.

1   Find your friend's post on your Profile.

2   Find the box marked "Write a comment..." and click the **sticker icon** to the right, highlighted next.

Write a comment...

3 A list of sticker categories will appear. The stickers are sorted by emotions, which makes it easy to find the sticker you want.

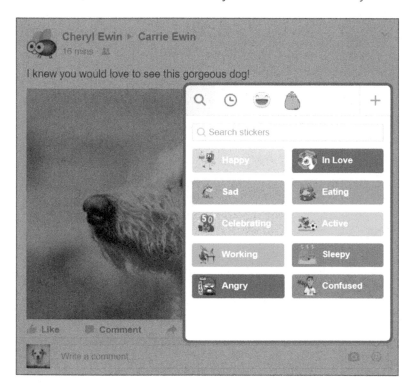

4 Choose a category. If the categories don't capture what you want to express, you can type a word or name into the search box above the categories (for example, "snow").

5 An array of fun stickers, like those to the right, will now appear.

6 Move your mouse over the stickers to reveal a scroll bar and click and drag the scroll bar up and down to see more stickers.

7 Click the sticker you want to use. The sticker will now be posted as a comment, as shown below.

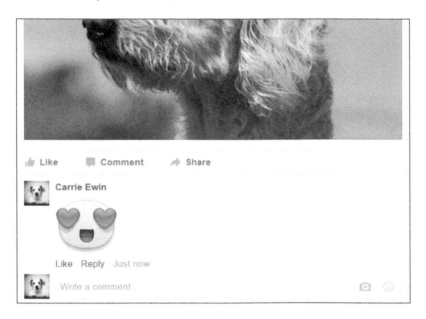

You might have noticed that some of the stickers move when you place your mouse over them. A select few of the stickers are animated, and they will move when you post them!

ACTIVITY #23

For this activity, find an old post on your Profile created by a friend.

1. Find and read the post that was added by your friend.

2. Write a comment in reply to the post.

3. Send a sticker that expresses your feelings.

Keeping Up with Friends Using News Feed

The fastest way to catch up with your friends' news is through the News Feed page. Remember from Lesson 1 that this is the page that loads automatically when you first log in to Facebook.

The News Feed page provides a snapshot of your friends' news. Facebook shows you only their most recent and popular posts on the News Feed page, so whenever you go to the News Feed page, it's updated with new activity from your friends. This is a brilliant way of quickly reading recent posts from your friends. If you have a lot of friends, though, you might see only a very small selection of posts from each one. To see the latest updates from a friend, it's often best to visit their Profile page.

To browse through the News Feed, follow these steps:

1 Click the **f** button to go to the News Feed page.

2 You will then see the News Feed page. Important and eventful posts from your friends will appear in the middle of the page, as shown on the next page.

3 Keep moving down the page to enjoy more posts!

Let's take a closer look at the types of posts you might see.

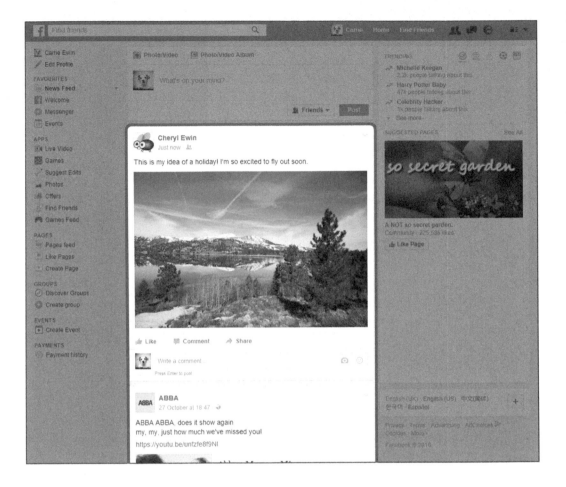

VIEWING TEXT AND PHOTO POSTS

Much of the time, posts that appear on your News Feed are those that a friend has posted to their own Profile. It might be just a text post, like this one.

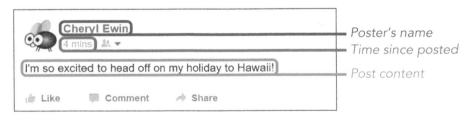

Poster's name
Time since posted
Post content

The post will include the following items:

* **The poster's information:** The name of the friend who made the post and their Profile picture.

* **The time since the post was created:** How long ago the post was made—this is useful so that you know current the post is.

* **The content of the post:** The post's message.

Some posts might be a photo post, like this one.

If the post has a photo, you can see it at full size by clicking the photo once. Click the X in the top-right corner of the photo to close it.

VIEWING VIDEO POSTS

Some posts may also contain a video, in which case the video will begin playing automatically when it appears on your page. Here are a few hints about videos:

* Click the speaker symbol to turn on the sound.

* Pause the video by clicking the play/pause button.

✳ Click the double-headed arrow to see the video full sized. Click it again to close the video.

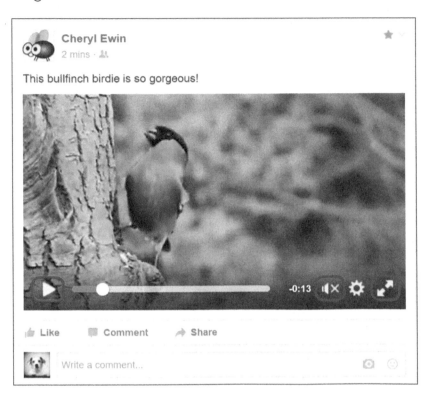

VIEWING WEB LINKS IN POSTS

Some posts contain links to web pages to share something interesting the poster has found. In these cases, the poster is usually encouraging you to click the link and view the web page for yourself.

> ✳ *WARNING: These links can sometimes contain viruses. Be wary about clicking links from people you don't know or in posts that look odd or suspicious. For example, if the text doesn't sound like something your friend would say, or the link doesn't look like something your friend would usually recommend, then it's best to avoid clicking it.*

A post with a web link will look something like this.

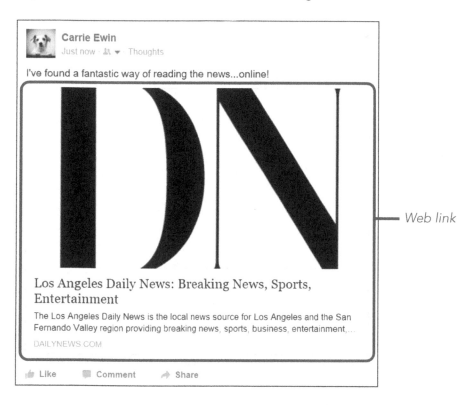

Web link

The web link appears beneath the written message in the post. Often a web link is accompanied by a small image or logo of the website and a short summary. If you want to visit the web page, simply click anywhere in the web link.

Phew, We Did It!

In this lesson, you learned to post on the Profile pages of your Facebook friends and to respond to posts on your Profile page. These skills will help keep you in contact with those nearest and dearest to you! In this lesson, you learned how to do the following:

* View a friend's Profile and explore the different sections

* Like, react to, and comment on a friend's posts

* Save a friend's photos

* Write a post on a friend's Profile

* Post pictures and videos on a friend's Profile

* View, like, react to, and comment on posts on your Profile

* Discover posts using the News Feed page

Excellent job! Now it's time to turn up the fun and learn to play games in the next lesson.

LESSON REVIEW

Congratulations, you've completed Lesson 7! Take this opportunity to review what you've learned by completing the following activities. If you can do so with confidence, you are ready for Lesson 8. If not, don't lose heart—just keep practicing!

1. View a friend's Profile.

2. Find a recent post on your friend's Profile that includes a photo you like.

3. Like and comment on the photo.

4. Add a photo or video on your friend's Profile.

LESSON 8
PLAYING GAMES

Now it's time to turn up the fun! In this lesson
you're going to learn to play games on Facebook.

Why Play Games on Facebook?

Facebook offers a huge number of games—many more than you could find in your living room! So whatever type of game you fancy playing, Facebook will have one for you. The following diagram shows some of the many types of games you can play on Facebook.

Most importantly, when you play a game on Facebook, you can play against other people without leaving the comfort of your sitting room. You can play against your Facebook friends or any one of the huge number of opponents (some games have millions!) from all over the world. This means you can play at any time of the day or night.

Playing games can also be an excellent way of connecting with friends and family and even making new Facebook friends.

BUT WHAT'S THE COST?

Most of the games on Facebook are free to play. This is excellent news, but in some cases there is a slight catch to be aware of: some games encourage or require you to pay as you progress. Here are some examples:

* **The game is free to play until you reach a certain level, but after that you have to pay to continue.** For example, you may play and enjoy a Sudoku game until you complete 20 puzzles, at which point you'll be asked to pay $3 to continue playing.

* **The game is free to play, but certain items in the game must be paid for.** In some cases, you need these items to advance in the game. For example, you may *play* the game for free, but you might not be able to win or improve your skills until you've paid $3 to buy your character an item, such as a new pair of boots, in the game.

It's important to note that most games are completely free without a catch and you will be given plenty of warning if payments are expected. Also, you must enter payment details to complete a payment, so you won't be able to make an accidental purchase.

THE NAME OF THE GAME IS PRIVACY!

Privacy in games is a little different than in other situations on Facebook because the games have been created by outside companies rather than Facebook itself. Facebook simply offers a great place to play the games. This means that games will not automatically have access to the information you've added to Facebook, so they'll often ask to access your information. Although this may sound a little worrying, there are great benefits to allowing this, such as being able to play against your Facebook friends.

When you first install a game, it may request access to the following types of information:

* **Publicly available information:** The game will usually request all the information you've made publicly available on your Profile, such as your name, Profile picture, cover photo, and gender.

* **Friends list:** Many games will request access to your list of Facebook friends. This lets the game give you the option to play against your friends and to share your scores. Unfortunately, it can mean that your friends receive annoying advertisements or notifications from the game on their Profiles.

* **Biographical information:** Many games will request access to the information you've added to your biography, such as your birth year, people or places you've chosen to like, and your email address. This information might be quite personal, so if you're uncomfortable with the information a game is asking to collect, think twice before setting up the game.

Meeting the Games Page

All the games on Facebook can be found on the Games page. This means you only need to go to one place to find them. To get to the Games page, follow these steps:

1 Click the **f** button to go to the News Feed page.

2 From the Side Menu, click **Games**, as shown on the next page.

* NOTE: *If you created your Facebook account between 2015 and early 2016, and if you are using Facebook on Internet Explorer or Microsoft Edge, then your Side Menu may look a little different and the Games button may appear in a slightly different spot.*

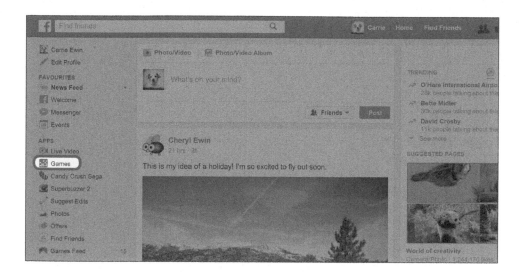

3. The Games page will then display, as shown next. The Games page looks quite busy, but it's actually very easy to find your way around, as you'll soon see.

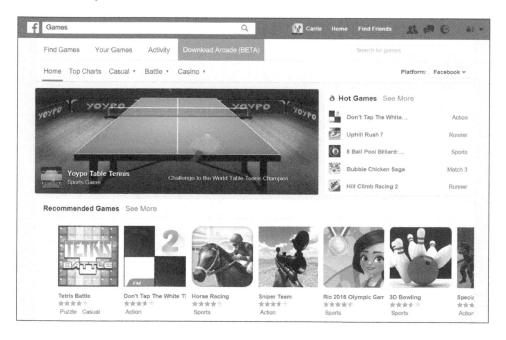

Finding Games

Facebook has lots of great games, but you need to find them first! You have three methods of finding games on Facebook:

* **By category:** If you know you want to play a particular type of game (such as a card game) but you don't have a specific game in mind, you can search by category.

* **By name:** If you know the name of a particular game, you can search for it by name.

* **By browsing popular games:** If you want to try out games that many other Facebook users have enjoyed, you can browse through the most popular and recommended games.

As you can see, you don't need to know what you want to play before you start. Facebook lets you browse everything that's available, and you can try whatever you like the look of.

Find games by category.   Find games by name.   Find popular games.

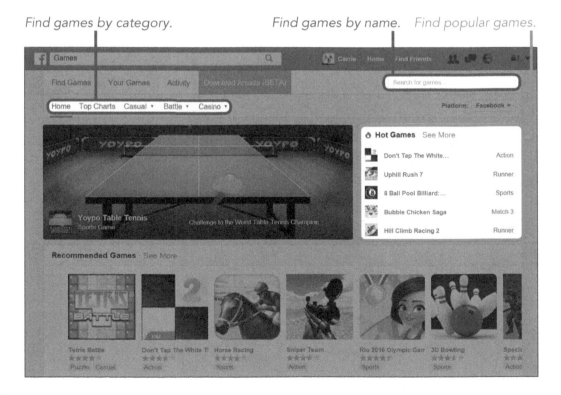

FINDING GAMES BY CATEGORY

Sometimes you know you want to play a certain type of game, such as a card game or a word game, but aren't sure which game in particular. You can search by category or genre and see what Facebook has to offer! Facebook splits games into three broad categories, and from there you can find games of more specific genres.

1. At the top of the screen, find the Casual, Battle, and Casino categories highlighted here.

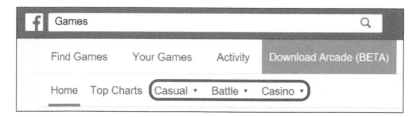

* **Casual:** These are quick, casual games you can pick up and then put down until you're ready to play again. The genres in this category include puzzle games, board games, matching games, card games, word games, and more.

* **Battle:** These games often take longer to complete and are played against another Facebook user. The genres in this category include action games, role-playing games, strategy games, sports games, and more.

* **Casino:** Casino games include slots, poker, table games, and bingo.

2. Click the category of game you would like to play. For now, just try Casual.

3. A list will appear with some further game genres. From the drop-down list, click the genre of game you'd like to play. In this case, try puzzle games, highlighted next.

4   A list of games will appear, like the one shown here. This list changes frequently, so you will probably see something a little bit different on your screen.

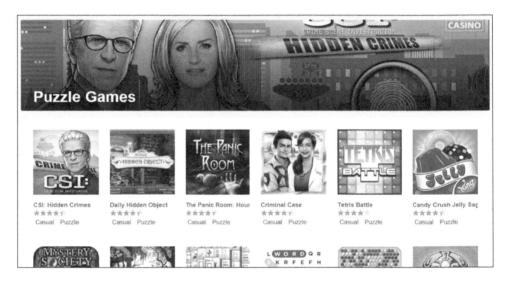

Each little picture represents a game, with the name and some other information listed underneath. The information here will help you decide what type of game you've found and whether it is a match for you. Let's look at Tetris Battle (shown to the right) as an example.

Tetris Battle
★★★★☆
Casual   Puzzle

* The game picture (known as a *tile*) has a background image of Tetris cubes with the heading Tetris Battle.

* The name of the game also appears underneath the tile.

* The number of stars underneath the game's name demonstrates how popular the game is. The more blue stars you see, the more popular the game is.

* Underneath the stars, you can see the categories under which this game has been classified.

To learn more about a game, you can click its game tile, but we'll get to that a little later after you've mastered searching for a game.

ACTIVITY #24

In this activity, you'll practice searching for games by category.

1. Open the Games page.

2. Find the game WordCrack by searching through the categories of games. (As a hint, WordCrack is played by putting certain letters together to make as many words as possible.)

FINDING GAMES BY NAME

You might want to play a particular game or find a game you know your Facebook friends are also playing. You might also have heard about a popular game that you can't wait to try! In such cases, you can search for the game by name directly.

1 Click in the game search box, highlighted below. The game search box appears below the Facebook Toolbar and should not be confused with the Facebook search box that appears higher up!

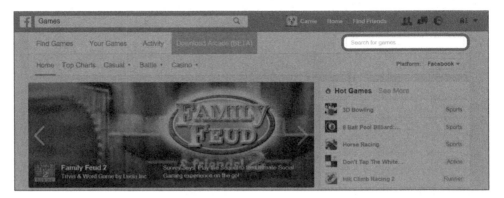

2 Type in the name of the game. Facebook will try to recognize the name. Click the correct game name from the list that Facebook provides. For this example, try to find the popular game Candy Crush Saga, as shown here.

3 The Facebook page for the game will then appear, as shown on the next page.

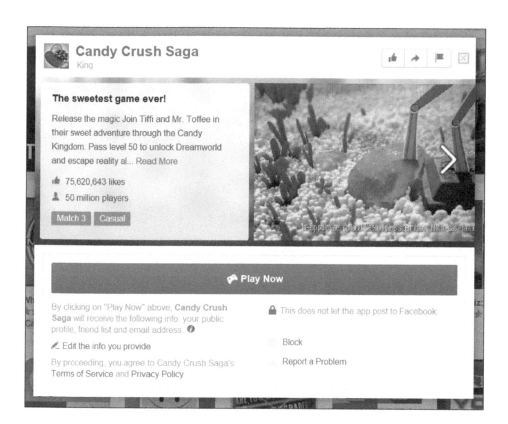

4 If you decide that you don't want to play this game, click the X in the top-right corner to return to the Games page.

ACTIVITY #25

In this activity, you'll practice searching for games by name.

1.   Open the Games page (if it's not already open).

2.   Find the game Mahjong by searching for it by name.

3.   Open the Mahjong game Facebook page and then close it by clicking the X.

As a hint, here is what the tile for the game looks like:

Mahjong
Game

FINDING GAMES BY POPULARITY

Popular games are often some of the very best games Facebook has to offer! They are also more likely to be played by your Facebook friends, so it's worth seeing what games are most popular.

1   Click **Top Charts** at the top of the Games page, as shown here.

2   A list of the most popular games will then appear. A blue number appears in the top-left corner of each game to show the game's popularity. For example, Candy Crush Saga is the number 1 most popular game, as shown next.

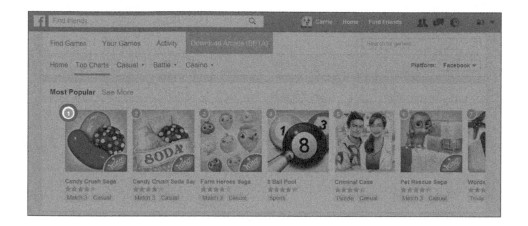

3 Click **See More** if you would like to see a longer list of the most popular games.

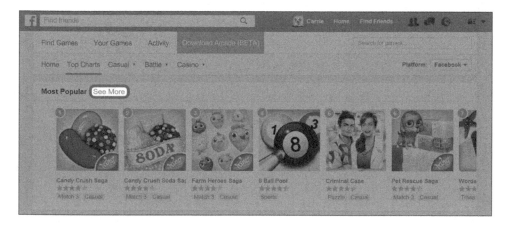

Setting Up a Game

Before you can play a game, you need to set it up. Setting up a game is not hard at all! It just involves adding an easy link to the game on your Profile, so you can start playing more quickly, and allowing the game to access some of your information. To set up a game, follow these steps:

1 Find the game you want to play and click the game tile. For this example, try out Candy Crush Saga, shown next. You can type the name into the game search box, find it through the categories, or browse through the most popular games until you find it.

2 A box containing information about the game will then pop up on the screen. You'll see a description of the game, which can help you decide whether you want to play it. At the bottom of the box you'll also see privacy information, which describes the personal information the game requires from your Facebook account.

A description of the game

A description of your personal information that the game will receive

3 The following figure highlights the large Play Now button. By clicking it, you're agreeing to let the game have the personal information described, so make sure you've read that information and are happy to agree.

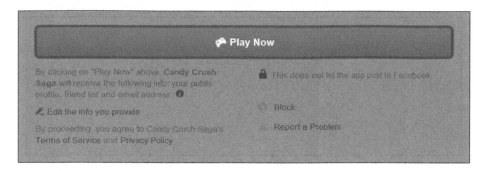

4 When you're ready, click **Play Now**.

5 You will then be taken to another screen where the game will load. Congratulations, you're ready to play!

Playing the Games You Love

To learn the ropes of playing a game, you'll first learn to play Candy Crush Saga! Candy Crush Saga is one of the most popular games on Facebook. You'll be presented with a grid of candies, and the aim is to get three of the same candies lined up in a row by switching candies with their neighbors. When three of the same candies are grouped together, they will burst and give you points. If you get enough points, you can progress to the next level.

1 Allow the game a few moments to load and then click the **Play** button when it appears, as shown on the next page.

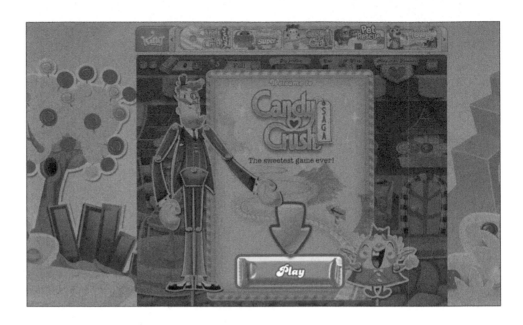

2 Level 1 will then load!

3 When you first begin to play, an assistant will appear to help you, as shown here.

Swipe this candy to the left to match 3 of the same!

Follow his instructions to learn to play. To move the candies, click the red candy with your left mouse button held down and drag it over the top of the purple candy and let go. The candies will then switch places. Candies can only be swapped with their direct neighbors above or below or to either side, not diagonally.

4   Continue following the assistant's instructions and switching candies until the assistant ends his introduction. When you're done with the introduction, click **Continue**.

5   Go ahead and play! Remember, your aim is to switch around candies to get three of the same type in a row. If you get stuck and hesitate for a couple of seconds, Candy Crush Saga will recommend the next move by highlighting candies you can switch, as shown on the next page.

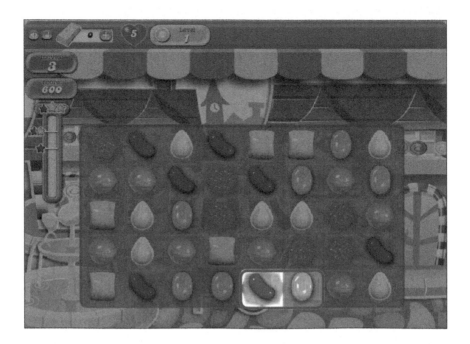

6 Keep switching candies until you've completed Level 1. You'll then see a screen like the one shown here.

7 Click **Next** to continue to Level 2.

Congratulations! You've just played one of the most popular games on Facebook. Only 2,605 more levels to go!

ACTIVITY #26

In Activity #25, you found the game Mahjong. Now you'll play it!

1. Search for Mahjong again.

2. Set up Mahjong by clicking **Play Now**.

3. Read the instructions to learn to play the game (or click **Skip**).

4. Enjoy yourself by playing a few rounds of Mahjong!

Exiting a Game and Playing Again

It's not always obvious how to exit a game. Games want you to keep playing them! Rather than explicitly ending the game, you just navigate to a different page. Here's how:

1 Look at the top of your screen and locate the **f** button, highlighted on the next page.

2   Click the **f** button to exit the game and go to the News Feed page.

The game will exit, but Facebook will remember what level you were on. This way, when you decide to play again, you can continue at the level where you left the game. We'll look at how to return to a game next.

After you've played a game once, it's easy to return and continue playing. The good news is that you'll pick right back up where you left off, and you won't be returned to Level 1. When you set the game up, a little button for that game was placed on your News Feed page so you can quickly play again.

1   Go to the News Feed page.

2   You'll find all the games you've played listed in the Side Menu for easy access.

3   Find Candy Crush Saga and click it once.

4   The game will load so you can keep playing!

5 The game may encourage you to invite your friends to play or to send your friends extra moves. Some friends will appreciate this kind gesture, but if you think that this is too intrusive, you can click the X in the top-right corner of the box, as shown below.

ACTIVITY #27

In this activity, we're going to play and then exit Mahjong.

1. Return to the News Feed page.

2. Open Mahjong and play another round.

3. When you're done playing, exit Mahjong by going back to the News Feed page.

Deleting Your Old Games

If you lose interest in a game, you can delete it to stop it from cluttering up your Games section. The game won't be deleted forever from Facebook, so you can go back and set it up again if you want to, but deleting a game will save space and stop you from getting updates from the game on your News Feed.

1 Go to the News Feed page.

2 Find the game you would like to remove in the Side Menu.

3 Move your mouse on top of the game and find the small image of a cog next to the name of the game, as shown here. In some internet browsers, this may appear as three small dots to the right of the game name instead of a cog.

4 Click the cog and a small menu will appear.

5 Click **Remove App**, as shown to the right.

6 A box will appear asking you to confirm the removal of the app. Click **Remove**.

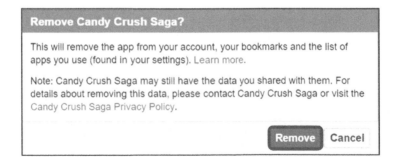

7 The game will now be removed from your Side Menu and your account.

Playing with a Friend

Not every game on Facebook allows you to play with a friend (for example, Candy Crush Saga is a game that you can only play alone), but some games do! To play with a Facebook friend, they will need to have set up the same game, and often they'll need to be logged in to Facebook and ready to play. If they haven't set up the game yet, you can invite them to do so, which we'll cover in a later section.

SETTING UP WORD BATTLE

We'll choose the popular game Word Battle as the example in this section. Word Battle is easy to play, so you can learn it quickly. To play, you just need to make one word out of nine letters. Each letter carries a value and your aim is to make the highest value word that you can in 40 seconds. To do this, you simply click each letter to form a word and wait until your time runs out and your score is calculated. You compete against a friend in four rounds, and the person with the highest score at the end wins the game! You both play at the same time, so you'll discover the winner at the end of four rounds.

To find and set up Word Battle, follow these steps:

1 Open the Games page and use the game search box to find the game Word Battle. Look for a game tile that looks like this:

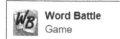

2 Click **Word Battle** from the drop-down list.

3 Set up the game by clicking **Play Now**.

4 Word Battle will load!

PLAYING WORD BATTLE WITH A FRIEND

Let's play! If you've exited Word Battle, open it again from the Side Menu on your News Feed page. Then follow these steps to play Word Battle with a friend.

1   If this is the first time you've played the game, an offer for a quick tour will appear. Click **Okay** to see how the game is played with the help of a tour guide. After the tour, you'll be encouraged to play a game and then you'll be returned to the game lobby.

2   Click **Create friend game**.

3   On the right side you'll see a list of friends you can challenge to Word Battle, as shown next. To appear on the list, a friend must also have Word Battle set up and currently open on their computer.

4   Find the friend you would like to play with and click **Add to game** next to their name. An invitation to play will now be sent.

5   If your friend accepts your invitation, they will appear as another player in the box next to yours, and the word *accepted* will appear next to their name.

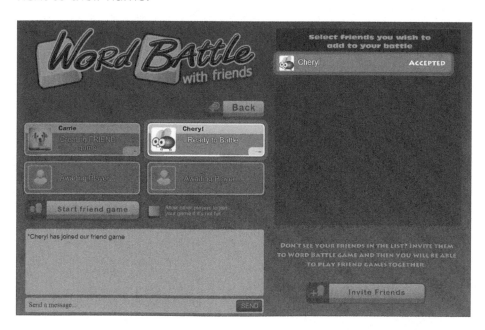

6 To begin the game, click **Start friend game** underneath the boxes with your names, as shown below.

7 The game will now begin! Click each letter to make your word and wait until your time runs out.

8 In one of the rounds you'll be asked to choose the type of letters you would like to play with (vowels or consonants). You can simply click **Random** to choose random letters.

9 At the end of the four rounds, the game will end and the scores will be calculated. Each friend will have a number next to their name indicating the order they placed in. In the following example, Carrie won and has a number 1 next to her name.

10 Click **Back To Lobby** to return to the game lobby, or click the **f** button to exit the game.

INVITING A FRIEND TO PLAY

If the name of the friend you would like to play doesn't appear on the battle list, then they probably don't have Word Battle set up. You can encourage them to set it up by following these instructions:

1 From the lobby of Word Battle, click **Invite Friends**.

2 Word Battle will request access to your friends list. Click **Continue as Your Name**.

3 Your friends list will then load. Check the box next to any friend that you would like to invite to play Word Battle, as shown on the next page, and then click **Send**.

4 A box will appear to confirm your invitation. Click **Send Request**, as shown below. Your friend request has now been sent!

More Great Games to Try

There are many wonderful games to try, and you should browse the categories and popular games to see what you like the look of. Try searching for games you like in real life, such as chess and solitaire;

there's often a digital version of most real-life games on Facebook. Here are some Facebook favorites:

* **8 Ball Pool:** A pool game you can play against your Facebook friends or random opponents.

* **Bingo Blitz:** Play Bingo against random opponents.

* **Candy Crush Soda Saga:** A follow-up to the original Candy Crush Saga, this game is only played against the computer.

* **Family Feud & Friends 2:** A trivia game based on the popular television game show *Family Feud*. You're given a question and must provide the most common answers. This game is played against random opponents and Facebook friends.

* **Solitaire Live:** Play a game of Klondike solitaire (otherwise known as patience) against a Facebook friend or random opponent. Both players play the same game at the same time. The first player to turn over all their cards wins.

* **Words with Friends:** This game is very similar to Scrabble. You use your letters to make words on a board and build upon previously played words. This game is played against your Facebook friends or random opponents.

Phew, We Did It!

In this lesson, you learned to play games on Facebook. These games should provide you many hours of entertainment with your nearest and dearest! We looked at how to:

* Explore the Games page

* Find games by category, name, and popularity

* Set up games

* Play games

* Exit and return to games

* Delete games

* Play with a friend

Brilliant! It's time to indulge your passions by joining Groups related to your interests in the next lesson.

LESSON REVIEW

Congratulations, you've completed Lesson 8! Take this opportunity to review what you've learned by completing the following activities. If you can do so with confidence, you are ready for Lesson 9. If not, don't lose heart—just keep practicing by playing more games!

1. Open the Games page.

2. Find the game Solitaire Arena.

3. Set up Solitaire Arena and play a game of solitaire.

4. After you've won a game, move on and play in a tournament.

5. Exit the game.

6. If you decide you don't like Solitaire Arena, delete it.

LESSON 9
GROUPS

In this lesson, you'll learn how to find and join interesting Facebook Groups.

With this lesson, you're holding the golden ticket into your new club! You'll learn how to search for a Group, choose the right one, join a Group, and participate in the Group's discussions with written posts and photos.

Why Would I Use a Facebook Group?

It can be hard at any age to find new people who share the same interests or hobbies as you do. With more than one billion users, Facebook is a great tool for connecting with people beyond your neighborhood.

Here's an example of one Group on Facebook.

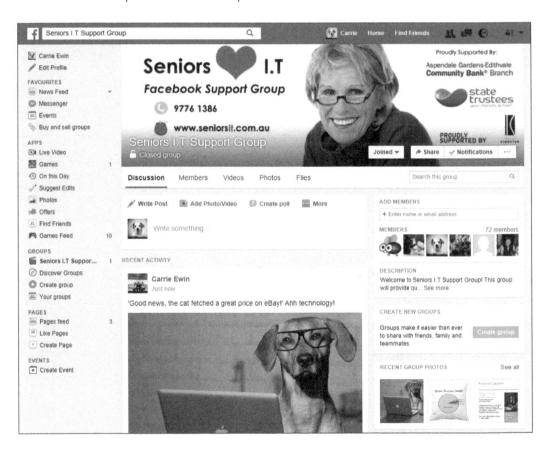

Just like a club, Facebook Groups will help you connect with people who can't wait to discuss your favorite hobby, show, location, person, or sport! You can find Groups on anything from sewing, traveling, or cars to your favorite movie. But unlike traditional clubs, a Facebook Group is actually a page dedicated to a particular topic where Group members can share things relevant to the Group. Even though you may never *meet* the other members of your Group, you will be able to enjoy discussions and share photos and videos together, all without leaving the comfort of your home.

And if you do want help connecting with people from a particular place, Facebook can help you find local Groups or even Groups of people who connect to your personal history, like graduates from your old high school. By joining these Groups, you can reconnect with old friends you haven't spoken to in years.

How Do I Protect My Privacy in Groups?

Protecting your privacy in Groups is important. In some Groups, you're sharing information with millions of strangers, so you want to be careful about what you provide. Facebook offers three Group privacy settings, and the setting is chosen by the creator of the Group. The type of privacy setting shows up under the Group name, like in the preceding example (a closed Group). We'll learn to find and identify the privacy setting of a Group later in this lesson. Here is a description of the three types of privacy settings:

* **Public Groups:** Public Groups are the most "open" type of Group and, therefore, the riskiest. *Everyone* can find and join them, and *everyone* can see what members post there. However, you still need to become a member of the Group to add a post. If you participate in a public Group, do not post personal or identifying information. For example, never post your contact information or pictures of the front of your house in a public Group.

* **Closed Groups:** Closed Groups have a medium level of privacy. *Everyone* can find the Group, but they must ask *permission* to join it. This provides a level of protection because the Group creator may refuse membership to a suspicious person. Most importantly, *only Group members can see posts in the Group.* This means that you can add a post in the Group and only other Group members will be able to read it. These Groups vary in terms of numbers and selectivity. Just like with public Groups, you need to become a member of the closed Group before you can add a post.

* **Secret Groups:** Secret Groups are the most secure. To find and join the Group, a person must be invited by the Group creator. This means that most Facebook users will never even know that the Group exists! This provides a great deal of security because the Group creator will only invite Facebook users who he or she knows are trustworthy. And as with closed Groups, *only* Group members can see posts in the Group or add posts to the Group.

Searching for Groups

Facebook has many, many Groups that will suit your interests or unite you with people who have something in common with you. But before you can start a discussion, you must first find a Group!

FINDING GROUPS BY GENERAL HOBBIES

If you have a general hobby, such as sports or food, rather than a very specific interest, then you may find it easier to discover Groups by category. This is a wonderful way to find Groups if you're not certain of what you would like to discuss. Here's how to find general Groups:

1 Open the News Feed page by clicking the **f** button.

2 From the Side Menu, click **Discover Groups**, as shown next.

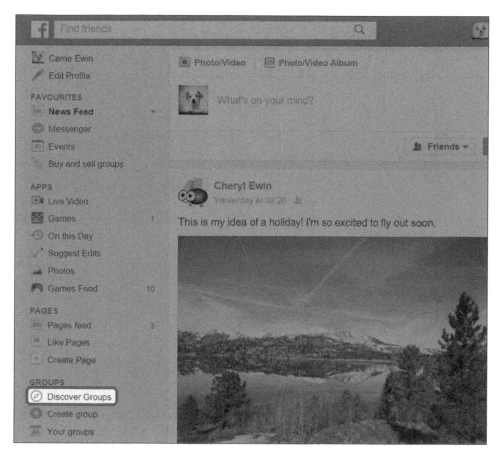

> **✳ NOTE:** *If your Side Menu looks a little different and you don't have a Discover Groups button, you may need to click Groups from the Side Menu.*

3 At the top of the page, you'll see different categories of Groups, as shown on the next page. These will each contain lots of Groups you might be interested in joining. Some categories, like Neighborhood & Community, will show local Groups near your neighborhood. You'll also find Groups for buying, selling, and professional networking in addition to hobby and interest Groups.

> **✳ NOTE:** *The categories are updated often, so yours may look a little different.*

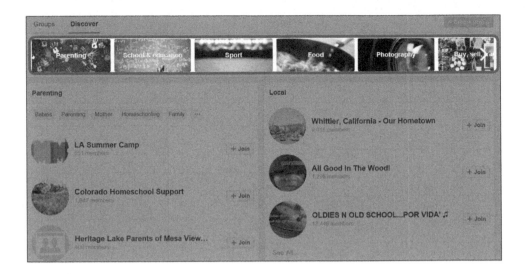

4 Click a category such as "Food."

5 A page full of relevant Groups will load, as shown below. Scroll down the page and look at the many Groups you might like to join!

FINDING GROUPS BY SPECIFIC INTERESTS

If you have specific interests, then you'll also be able to find the perfect Group for you! For example, if you would like to talk about beadwork, then you can find a Group discussing this.

Here's how to get started:

1 Click in the search box at the top of your screen.

2 Type in the name of your interest. You don't need to know the name of a Group; just type in something you are interested in. For this example, try typing in "beadwork and sewing."

3 A list of search results will appear, as shown below. You don't need to press ENTER!

Be aware that some of the results are *not* Facebook Groups. Sometimes advertisers create Facebook pages that look like Groups, so always look at the description under each result to find the word *Group*, as highlighted here.

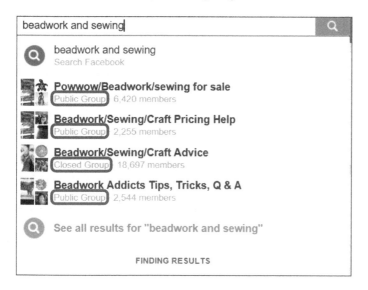

4 The list of results you see is just a small selection of the Groups that matched your search. To see more, press ENTER or click **See all results for "beadwork and sewing"** at the bottom of the search results, as shown in the previous figure. This will take you to a page of search results from every part of Facebook that matches the phrase "beadwork and sewing."

5 After all the results of your search have appeared, look at the top of the page and find a row of buttons to narrow down your search. Click **Groups** to show only Groups in your search results.

6 A long list of beadwork and sewing Groups on Facebook will now appear!

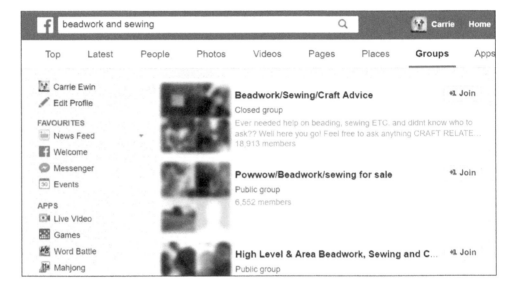

7 Read the name and short description of the Group to learn more about it and click the name of the Group to open it.

Group name

Number of members   *Group description*

ACTIVITY #28

In this activity, you'll find a Group that you might like to join. Here are the steps to follow:

1. Think of a hobby or subject you're interested in and search for a Group related to it using the search box. Some great examples are gardening, sewing, cooking, reading, and scuba diving.

2. Look carefully to see if any of your initial search results are Groups. If not, see more results and narrow them to Groups.

3. Find a Group that sounds like it shares your passion.

4. Write down the name of the Group.

Is This Group for Me?

There are so many Groups on Facebook that it can be difficult to decide if you've found the right one. We'll use the Beadwork/Sewing/Craft Advice Group in this section as an example of choosing a Group.

1 In the Facebook search box, type **Beadwork/Sewing/Craft Advice**.

2 Click the name of the Group from the list of results.

3 The Group page will then open, as shown below.

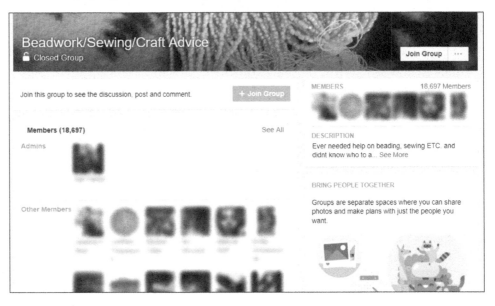

✱ NOTE: *When you view the page for a closed Group like Beadwork/ Sewing/Craft Advice, you won't be able to see members' posts until you become a member. This is why the Group page currently looks quite empty. After you join a Group, the page will be filled with discussion.*

After you've reached the Group page, you can find out more about the Group. Look for the following pieces of information to decide if the Group is a good match for you.

Group type   *Number of members*

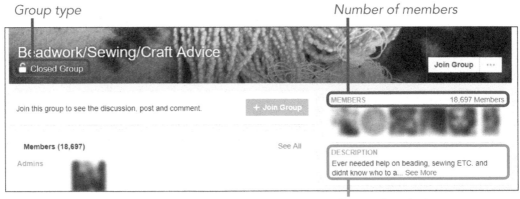

Group description

* **Group description:** This area tells you about the Group, its aims, and its target audience. If you can't see the entire description, click **See More** at the bottom of the description. If the Group is closed, the description may give some general guidelines as to the type of members the Group will accept.

* **Number of members:** Groups with many members (10,000 to 1,000,000) will usually be more active, and the conversations may be more stimulating. By contrast, Groups with smaller numbers may encourage you to ask more questions and build stronger connections with the Group members.

* **Group type:** This will help you learn more about the Group's privacy. Refer to "How Do I Protect My Privacy in Groups?" on page 187 to learn more about how open, closed, and public Groups protect their members and their posts.

ACTIVITY #29

In Activity #28, you found an interesting Group. In this activity, you'll explore this Group in more detail.

1. Search for the Group you wrote down in Activity #28.

2. Read the Group description. Does the Group discuss your interests? Is it aimed at your level of experience? Would you be comfortable discussing this topic with strangers? Check the number of members in the Group. Are there too few members to have a full discussion? Are there too many members for you to get to know them as well as you'd like?

(continued)

3. Check the type of Group. If the Group is public, think about whether you're comfortable with your posts being read by any Facebook user. If the Group is public, try reading some of the comments from other Group members and see how you feel about them.

4. Decide if you want to join the Group. Is there another Group you would prefer that also discusses this topic?

Joining a Group

Once you've found a Group you like the look of, you can become a member of it. If it's a closed Group, you'll need to ask to join, and then the Group administrator will decide whether to accept you. Only then will you be a member of the Group. The advantage of joining a Group is that you can add your views to the discussion by posting to the Group page. If it's a closed or secret Group, you will only be able to read the posts of other members after you've joined the Group.

1 Open the Group page of the Group you decided to join in Activity #29.

2 Click **Join Group** just underneath the title of the Group. If it's a closed Group, the Group administrator will review your request and decide if they would like to accept it and make you a member. You'll have to wait to proceed until the administrator approves your membership. This usually takes a couple of hours or days.

3   When your membership has been approved, a red number will appear on the notification button to indicate that you have a new notification. Click the **notification button**.

4   If you've been accepted into the Group, the notification will let you know. Congratulations!

5   Click the notification to be brought to the Group Page. Now that you're a member, you can see all the prior posts!

Let's Join the Discussion!

Now that you've joined the Group, it's time to join in the discussion!

POSTING TO A GROUP

You can post written comments and photos to the Group just like you can on a friend's Profile. To post to a Group, follow these steps:

1   Open the Group page of the Group you just joined.

2   Underneath the name and Group banner, click in the **Write Post** box, highlighted next.

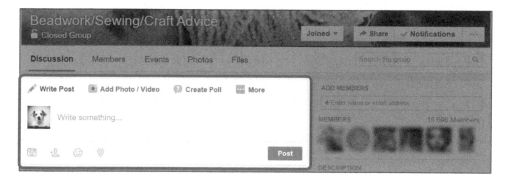

3   Write the question, thought, or idea you want to share with the Group, and when you're ready, click **Post**.

RECEIVING REPLIES TO YOUR POST

Groups are made for discussion, so you'll usually receive a reply to your post in a Group. Here's how to view a reply to your post:

1 A red number will appear on the notification button to indicate that you have a new notification. Click the **notification button**.

2 The notification will tell you that someone has commented on your post in the Group.

3 Click on the notification and you'll be taken to your post inside the Group. Underneath your post you can read the replies.

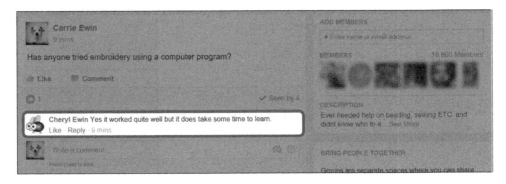

POSTING PHOTOS TO THE GROUP

After you've joined the Group, you can also post photos that you think the Group might enjoy. In a closed or secret Group, only members of the Group will be able to see the photos you post to the Group.

1 From the Group page, click in the **Write Post** box.

2 At the top of the box, click **Add Photo/Video**, as shown next.

3 Click **Upload Photos/Videos**, highlighted here.

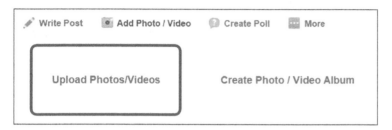

4 The File Explorer window will then open. Find the picture or video on your computer, click on it, and then click **Open**.

5 Your photo or video will then appear in the bottom-left corner of your post. It will look very small before you post it.

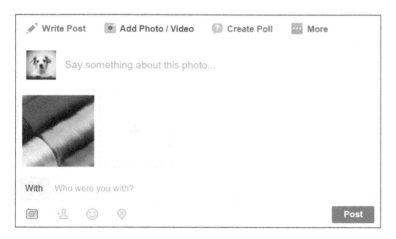

6 To add a message, click the words "Say something about this photo…" and type in your accompanying message.

7 Click **Post** to post the picture and the message to the Group.

RESPONDING TO GROUP POSTS

You can also join the discussion by commenting on or replying to the post of another Group member. This can be a great way of continuing the conversation! Of course if you would prefer not to write a reply, you can simply like or react to the post. You can also respond to a Group post with a cute sticker to sum up your feelings instead of using words! You learned these skills in Lesson 7 and we'll review them using Groups now.

Commenting on a Post

To leave a written comment, often called a reply, follow these steps:

1   From the Group page, find a post you think is interesting by another Group member.

2   Click in the **Write a comment...** box at the bottom of the post.

3   Type your comment and press ENTER on your keyboard to post it.

4   Your reply will now appear underneath the original post.

Commenting on a Post Using a Sticker

You can also spice up your reply to a post using a sticker. To reply with a sticker, follow these steps:

1   Find the box marked "Write a comment..." at the bottom of the post. To the right of this box, click the **sticker icon**, as shown next.

2 Click the category that matches your feelings to open the sheet of stickers. If the categories don't capture what you want to express, you can click in the search box above the categories and type a word (for example, "excited").

3 Click your chosen sticker.

4 Your sticker will then appear underneath the post.

Liking and Reacting to a Post

You can like a post to let everyone know you agree with the comment. If you feel more strongly, you can react to a post, which is similar to liking a post but you have a range of reactions to choose from.

1 To like a post, click the **Like** button at the bottom of the post.

2 To choose a reaction, move your mouse over the Like button and hold it there for a few seconds without clicking. A list of reactions will appear in the form of pictures.

3 Click the reaction that you'd like.

4 Your reaction and name will appear just underneath the post. Other Group members will be able to see your name and your reaction.

ACTIVITY #30

In this activity, you're going to like an earlier post in the Group you joined.

1. From the Group page, find a post that has been written recently by a member of the Group.

2. Read the post to see if you agree with it. If so, click **Like**!

Staying Current with Groups

There are two main ways to learn about new posts in a Group:

* **News Feed:** After you become a member of a Group, new posts in the Group will appear in your News Feed. This helps you keep track of what's going on in the Group. Make sure to check your News Feed regularly to view these posts!

* **Visit the Group:** By visiting the Group, you will see all the most recent posts and comments made by members of the Group. This is the best way to stay up to date on what's happening.

You can visit a Group as often as you want using the steps below:

1 Open the News Feed page by clicking the **f** button.

2 From the Side Menu, find **Groups**. Notice that under the Groups heading is a list of the Groups that have currently accepted you as a member.

3 Click the name of the Group, and the Group Page will open.

4 You can now read the latest posts and photos!

> * **NOTE:** *If you have the Side Menu shown below, the Groups you've joined will appear in the Shortcuts section. If you can't see the Group, click **See More** at the bottom of the Shortcuts list to reveal it.*

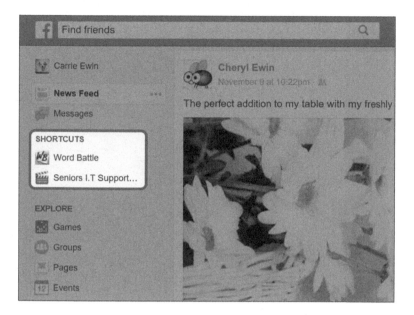

Unfollowing and Leaving Groups

You might find that the number of posts on your News Feed from a particular Group becomes annoying but that you would like to stay a member of the Group to participate in discussions. In this case, you can turn off the Group posts to your News Feed but still stay a member of the Group. To do this, follow these steps:

1 Open the Group page from the News Feed page.

2 Click **Joined** to the right of the Group name.

3   A small menu will appear. Click **Unfollow Group**.

You'll now no longer see posts from the Group on your News Feed, but you can still open the Group page at any time and read the posts.

The time may come when you want to leave a Group, if you no longer have any interest in discussing the topic or if the Group wasn't what you expected it to be.

1   Open the Group page from the News Feed page.

2   Click **Joined**.

3   A small menu will appear. Click **Leave Group**.

4   You will see a message asking you to confirm that you wish to leave the Group. Click **Leave Group**.

The Group page will then reload and you will no longer be a member. If the Group is closed or secret, you won't be able to read posts in the Group anymore.

Phew, We Did It!

In this lesson, you learned to join Groups on Facebook. Groups will keep you conversing about your favorite topics and passions with fellow fans all over the globe!

You learned how to:

* Find Groups that match your broad hobbies

* Find Groups that match your specific interests

* Choose and join a Group

* Post to a Group

* Receive a reply in a Group

* Post photo posts to a Group

* Reply to, like, and react to posts

* Unfollow and leave a Group

Well done! In the next lesson you'll learn how to have private conversations with friends.

LESSON REVIEW

Congratulations, you've completed Lesson 9! Take this opportunity to review what you've learned by completing the following activities. If you can do so with confidence, you are ready for Lesson 10. If not, don't lose heart—just keep practicing!

1. Search for the Group called "Seniors Love Facebook."

2. Open the Group.

3. The Group is a closed Group. Once you're certain that you've found the correct Group, ask to join!

(continued)

4. After your membership has been accepted, add a written post introducing yourself to the Group. Tell the Group why you love Facebook and what you would like to learn more about.

5. Find an earlier post and write a reply to stimulate conversation.

6. Visit the Group often to read new posts!

LESSON 10
MESSENGER AND CHAT

In this lesson, you'll learn how to send and receive Facebook messages. You'll also learn how use Chat to have live, private conversations with Facebook friends.

Why Converse on Facebook?

Facebook is a fantastic place for conversations! It's free whether you're conversing with someone halfway across the globe or your next-door neighbor. Even better, Facebook Messenger allows you to send and receive responses instantly. No waiting around for mail deliveries! Best of all, Facebook makes it easy to converse with a wide range of friends and family—from those you talk to regularly, to those you haven't spoken with in years. With Messenger, you don't need an address or a telephone number, so you can even contact people you've fallen out of touch with.

Messages are private and can only be seen by you and the person you're writing with. Think of a message like an email: you send your message and simply wait for your friend to read it and send a response. As with Facebook posts and comments, you can also include photos, videos, and stickers for added personality. Messenger is a wonderful way to converse on Facebook when you only want yourself and the recipient to read the message.

Facebook Chat lets you have a written conversation with someone on Facebook "live" or in "real time." It's more like chatting in person or on the telephone. For this reason, you can begin a Chat only if both you and your friend are on Facebook at the same time and are able to respond to each other. As with Messenger, you can also send photos and stickers to keep the conversation flowing.

You can even send and receive messages and Chat conversations with people who are not your Facebook friends. This can be useful if you want to introduce yourself to someone before requesting their friendship or share messages with someone that you wouldn't want to add as a Facebook friend. If you send a message or Chat to someone you're not friends with, that person will receive a message request that they can accept or decline. This gives them the chance to ignore your message and you'll never know that they've seen it! A person who is not your friend can also begin conversations with you. If you receive a message request, simply click the request to read the message and then choose to accept or decline the request. If you accept, you won't become Facebook friends but you will be able to converse! In this lesson we'll focus on conversing with your Facebook friends, but remember that you can follow the same steps to converse with a person who is not your friend.

Facebook Messenger

You'll send and receive messages using Messenger, which is a page on Facebook dedicated to private messages. Follow these steps to open Messenger:

1 Open the News Feed page by clicking the **f** button.

2 Click the **Messenger** button from the Side Menu, shown next.

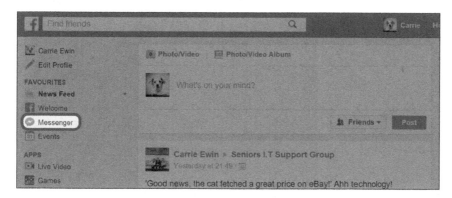

✽ NOTE: *If you created your Facebook account between 2015 and early 2016, and if you are using Facebook on Internet Explorer or Microsoft Edge, then your Side Menu may look a little different and the Messenger button may appear in a slightly different spot.*

*You might also see the Messages button instead. This button opens the Message Center, which looks slightly different from Messenger but does almost all the same things, so you can still follow along with this lesson. However, if you'd like to try Messenger, simply open your internet browser and type **www.messenger.com** into the address bar at the top. Messenger will then open!*

3 Messenger will open. If you haven't sent or received any messages yet, it will be empty, like this:

If you've recently become friends with someone, their name may appear on the side to encourage you to begin a conversation. This is Facebook's way of encouraging you to say hello!

4 You may also receive a heartwarming welcome from Messenger, as shown below. This message explains that Messenger is actually stored on a different website from Facebook and that you've now left the Facebook website. Don't worry—you can return to Facebook at any time. Click **OK**.

Welcome to Messenger

Now all of your messages can be viewed on Messenger.com. We think it's a better way to message from your computer, and we'll keep working to improve it. You can also keep chatting on Facebook.

OK

Let's take a closer look at how Messenger will look after you've sent and received a few messages.

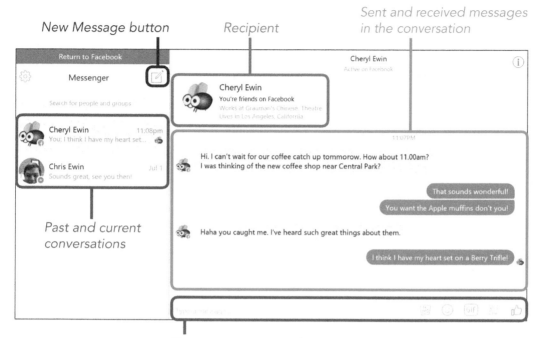

New Message button   Recipient   Sent and received messages in the conversation

Past and current conversations

Type a new message box

* **Past and current conversations:** The names and Profile pictures of the friends you've shared private messages with will appear in the left column. This section also shows the first few words of the most recent message and the time that message was sent. If you want to send another message to someone in this list, or read earlier messages, just click that person's name and your conversation will appear on the right.

* **Sent and received messages in the conversation:** The messages sent back and forth between you and your Facebook friend will appear on the right. These conversations are saved so you can go back and read old messages.

* **Recipient:** This area shows which Facebook friend you've shared these messages with.

* **Type a new message box:** The box at the bottom of the page is where you can write your next message to your friend.

* **New Message button:** Click the New Message button at the top of the page to begin a private message conversation with a friend.

SENDING A MESSAGE

You're always able to privately message any friend on Facebook without needing any extra information such as an email address or a telephone number! Remember, the message will only be seen by your friend and yourself. Follow these steps to send a new message:

1 Click the **New Message button**.

2 Click in the **To** box and type the name of the friend you wish to message.

3 As you type, Facebook will try to recognize your friend. Click the correct name from the list that Facebook provides.

4 If you want to send the message to more than one friend, you can create a group message by typing in a second name and clicking the correct name from the list that Facebook provides. This will allow all the recipients in the group to read your message and read any replies from every other recipient. You can add as many people as you like in this way.

5 When you have your recipients set, click in the **Type a message...** box at the bottom of the page.

6 Type a message to your friend(s). You can write as many messages as you like, so your first message doesn't have to be as long as *War and Peace*!

7 When you're ready, click **Send** to send your message.

8 Your sent message will now appear in the middle of the page. The time that you sent it will appear just above the message, as shown below. Your friend(s) can now see this message!

＊ NOTE: *You might also notice that when you send a message to a friend, some options appear on the right. These options are rarely used; click the **i** button in the top-right corner to remove them.*

ACTIVITY #31

In this activity, you're going to send a message to a friend or family member with an invitation.

1. Pick a friend or family member you'd like to catch up with.

2. Start a new message and add your friend as the recipient.

3. Write and send your message.

Notice that the message you sent earlier in this lesson hasn't disappeared! Your previous conversation will appear when you click their name from the left column of Messenger.

SENDING PHOTOS AND VIDEOS

Just like with written messages, you might prefer to send some photos and videos privately. This is an excellent idea for photos that have some significant meaning to you and one other person (like photos of your grandchildren), or for fun moments that only involved a few others.

To send a photo or video, follow these steps:

1 Create a message by clicking the recipient's name from the left column of Messenger or by creating a new message and choosing a recipient.

2 From the "Type a message..." box, click the **add files button**.

3 The File Explorer window should open. Find the picture or video you want to send. Click it and then click **Open**.

4 Your photo or video will be sent, as shown below.

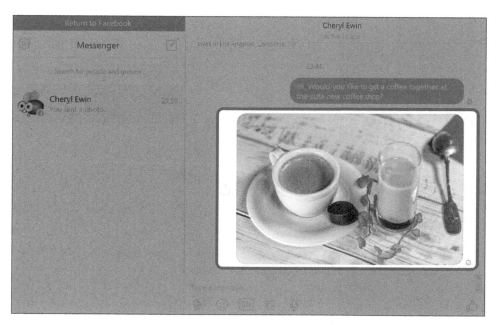

SENDING STICKERS AND GIFS

You can also do other fun things to personalize messages. One common way of spicing up your messages, and expressing how you feel, is to add a sticker like we did in Lesson 7. Another fun option is to send a *GIF*, a very short, moving picture sequence. GIFs are a popular way to express yourself!

Follow these steps to add a sticker:

1 From the "Type a message..." box, click the **sticker button**.

2 A list of sticker categories will appear. Stickers are sorted by category to make it easier to find the one you want!

3 If the categories don't capture the emotion you want, or if you have a specific sticker in mind, then you can type something else into the search box above the sticker categories.

4 Click the sticker to immediately send it to your friend.

5 Your sticker will be sent.

To send a GIF, follow these steps:

1 From the "Type a message..." box, click the **GIF button**.

2 A list of GIFs will appear. Scroll through the list of popular GIFs or use the search box to find a specific GIF of a particular item or emotion.

3 When you've found a great GIF, click it to send it to your friend. It will appear in the middle of the screen.

ACTIVITY #32

In this activity, you'll send a new message to a Facebook friend with either a sticker or a photo.

1. Create a new message and choose the recipient (maybe choose a different friend from those you've already written messages to in this lesson).

2. Type and send a message about something you're happy about.

3. Choose a sticker to express your happiness or send a photo of something that makes you happy.

4. Go back to Facebook.

READING AND RESPONDING TO MESSAGES

Of course, you're not the only one who can start a conversation! Your friends can send you messages too. In this section, we'll assume that you'll receive a message while you're enjoying Facebook. If you're still on the Messenger website, open up Facebook! When someone sends you a message, you'll receive a notification and a red number will appear on the message notification button.

1 Click the **message notification button**.

2   A notification will appear with the name and Profile picture of the friend who sent the message and the first few words of the message itself. The number in parentheses after the sender's name indicates how many messages the person has sent that you haven't read. The most recent message will be at the top.

3   Click the notification to open the message in a Messages Box, which will appear at the bottom of the page, as shown next.

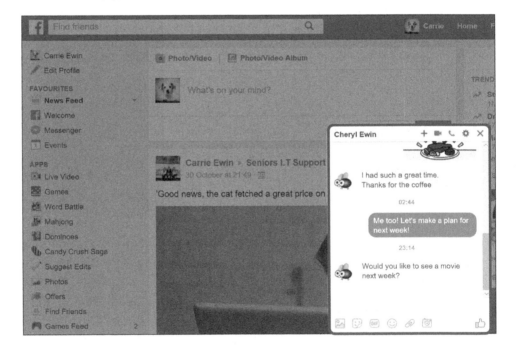

4 The Messages Box is different from the full Messenger and is a quicker way to read a message and send a response. Unfortunately, because it's quite small, it doesn't have some helpful features that Messenger has (such as a Send button!).

5 To reply using this quick box, click in the **Type a message...** box and type a message. When you're ready, press ENTER to send your message.

6 If you would rather open Messenger and reply from there (highly recommended), go to the News Feed page and click **Messenger** from the Side Menu, or use the address bar at the top of your screen to go to **www.messenger.com**.

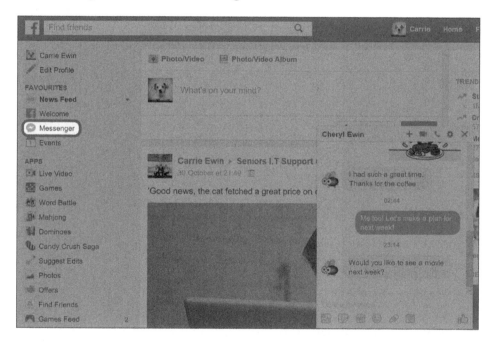

7 Click the correct conversation from the list on the left. It will open with your friend's most recent message at the bottom, as shown on the next page.

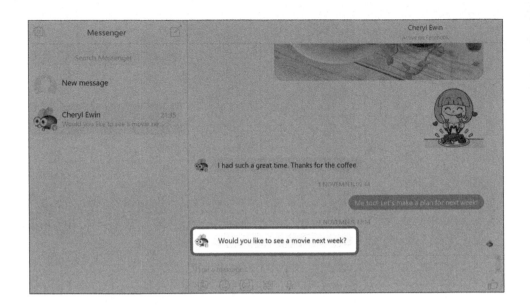

8   To reply, click in the **Type a message...** box and type your response. When you're ready, click **Send**, as shown below.

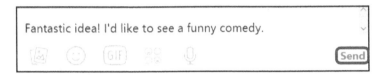

Fantastic idea! I'd like to see a funny comedy.

Send

9   Your reply will now appear, as shown here.

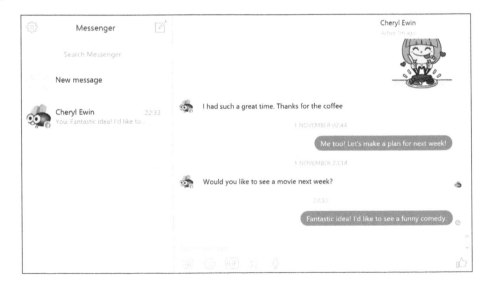

10 You can also reply with photos, videos, and stickers, just as you sent them before. Have a glance back at "Sending Photos and Videos" on page 215 and "Sending Stickers and GIFs" on page 216 to refresh your memory.

ACTIVITY #33

For this activity, you need to wait for a friend to message you first—or even better, ask someone to send you a Facebook message to get you started.

1. Keep an eye out for a new message notification.

2. When you get a notification, open the message in Messenger and get ready to reply!

3. Send a sticker that includes the word "thanks."

Lights, Camera, Chat!

Chat lets you have a live, real-time written conversation with someone on Facebook! When you're chatting, you and your friend are sending and answering messages in the moment, rather than leaving a message and waiting hours or days for a response. It's a bit like talking with a person beside you as opposed to sending them a letter.

While the mechanics of Chat and Messenger are very similar, the key difference is that a conversation through Messenger occurs when one person is not necessarily signed in to Facebook. The message sits and waits until the person connects to Facebook, reads the message, and responds. A Chat conversation happens when both people are connected to Facebook and ready to chat. The message is read and generally responded to instantly.

FINDING THE CHAT LIST

In order to use Chat, you need to know who is signed in to Facebook at the same time as you. Fortunately, Facebook makes this easy by providing a list of friends who are signed in and potentially available for you to chat with. The way your Chat List appears will depend on the size of your web browser, but it will always appear on the right side of your page no matter where you are on Facebook. To locate your Chat List, follow these steps:

1 Look at the bottom-right corner of your screen. If you see a bar that says "Chat," like the one highlighted next, click it.

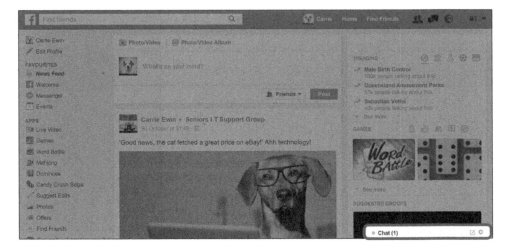

A list of friends who may be available to chat will pop up, as shown here.

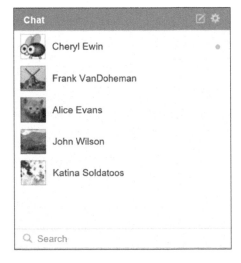

2 If your screen is larger, your Chat List will look like a column of names along the right side of your screen, as shown next, instead of a bar in the bottom-right corner.

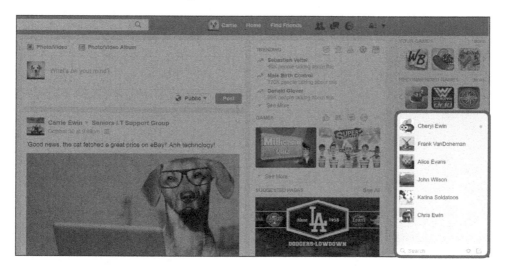

MEETING THE CHAT LIST

There's a lot of information in your Chat List, so let's take a closer look at what you'll see.

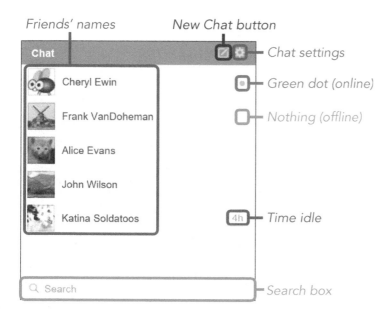

Friends' names

New Chat button

Chat settings

Green dot (online)

Nothing (offline)

Time idle

Search box

NOTE: *If your Chat List appears as a bar along the bottom of the page, make sure to click it to open it now if it isn't already open.*

* **Friends' names:** A list of your friends will appear on your Chat List. If a friend is connected to Facebook and ready to chat, you can click their name to begin a Chat conversation.

* **New Chat button:** This button will open a new Chat and give you the option to chat with anyone on Facebook, even if they're not your friend. To begin a new Chat in this way, click the New Chat button and type the name of the person you would like to chat with into the To field. Facebook will try to recognize the name, and you can click on the correct name from the list.

* **Chat settings:** The cog icon shows the Chat settings menu. These settings usually don't need to be changed, so we won't explore this button.

* **Green dot:** Friends with a green dot next to their name are currently signed in to Facebook and able to chat.

* **Nothing:** If a friend has neither a green circle nor a number next to their name, then they are not signed in to Facebook and probably won't respond.

* **Time idle:** If a friend has a number followed by *m*, *h*, or *d* next to their name, they're signed in to Facebook but may not be available to chat. The number indicates the amount of time they have been signed in but not using Chat. An *m* indicates the number of minutes, *h* the hours, and *d* the days. If this number is large, the friend has probably been idle for a long time and may not reply.

NOTE: *A lot of people leave themselves signed in to Facebook while they go about their day. If someone doesn't respond to your Chat messages, that's not necessarily a snub! They may just be signed in on their cell phone while they're at work, and are not immediately available.*

✳ **Search box:** If you have lots of friends currently online, they may not all fit on the list! To check whether a particular friend is connected to Facebook and ready to begin a chat, just type their name into the search box and click that person when they appear in the search list.

ENJOYING A CHAT CONVERSATION

Let's start a Chat:

1 Click the name of a friend with a green dot to begin a Chat conversation.

2 The Chat Box will open. You might notice that any prior Messenger conversations with your friend can be carried on in Chat. This is because Messenger and Chat are two halves of the same whole.

3 Now you can begin your conversation! Click in the **Type a message...** box at the bottom of the Chat Box (highlighted here).

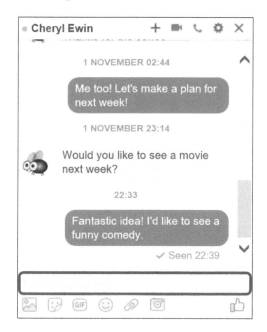

4   Type a Chat message. Because this is in real time, you'll probably want to write shorter messages than you would in a private message, to give your recipient a chance to respond.

5   When you're ready to send your message, press the ENTER key on your keyboard. Your message will appear in a blue bubble, as shown next.

6   When you receive a reply, a red number will appear on the message notification button in the Facebook Toolbar and the Chat Box will automatically reopen with your conversation and show your friend's latest reply. This is a handy advantage of Chat that means you can't miss a message!

7   When you're finished with the conversation for the time being, click the X on the right side of the box. This will close down the Chat Box. Remember, if the other person sends another Chat message, the box will automatically reopen.

ACTIVITY #34

In this activity, you're going to converse with a friend using Chat.

1. Wait until a friend you know well comes online and is shown with a green dot in your Chat List.

2. When they're available, begin a Chat conversation.

3. Try writing a message, sending an image, and sending a sticker.

4. Enjoy your replies.

5. Use your Chat conversation to organize another time to chat again!

Exploring Video Calling

One exciting feature of Facebook is the opportunity to share video calls with Facebook friends. A video call lets you see and speak to the person live. It's similar to sharing a telephone call, except you can also see the person—and the calls are free! To share a video call with a Facebook friend, you'll need to open Facebook using Google Chrome, Mozilla Firefox, or Opera. If you're not sure whether you have any of these, check for the following symbols on your computer desktop or in your Start menu:

Google Chrome

Mozilla Firefox

Opera

Unfortunately, Microsoft Edge and Internet Explorer don't support video calling. If you don't have Google Chrome, Mozilla Firefox, or Opera, you can download any of these browsers for free using the internet and then install it on your computer. Before you can video call, you'll also need to set up a web camera, microphone, and speakers so you can see and hear the other person and they can see and hear you. If you have a laptop computer or a tablet computer, these items are probably built in, but if you're using a desktop computer, you may need to purchase them.

To begin a video call, you need to begin a Chat conversation with a friend who's currently online and then click the **video camera icon** at the top of the Chat Box. Easy!

You might have also noticed the telephone icon next to the video camera icon. If you would prefer to share an audio call, where you can talk to each other but can't see each other, click this icon!

Phew, We Did It!

In this lesson, you learned to converse on Facebook using Messenger and Chat. Both Messenger and Chat will keep you connected with your nearest and dearest, almost as though you're in the same room! You learned how to:

* Send and receive private messages

* Send photos and videos with Messenger

* Send stickers with Messenger

* Find friends who are signed in and ready to Chat

* Send and receive Chat messages

* Explore video chat

Great job! In the next lesson you'll use Facebook to have fun in real life by creating and responding to invitations to Events.

LESSON REVIEW

Congratulations, you've completed Lesson 10! Take this opportunity to review what you've learned by completing the following activities. If you can do so with confidence, then you are ready for Lesson 11. If not, don't lose heart—just keep messaging and chatting away!

1. Begin a Messenger conversation.

2. Add a close friend or family member as the recipient.

3. Write a message about your newfound skills.

4. Send a sticker to celebrate your new skills.

5. When you get a reply, carry on your conversation.

LESSON 11

EVENTS

In this lesson, you're going to learn to send and receive invitations to events such as birthday parties, anniversary celebrations, and retirement bonanzas using Facebook.

What Is a Facebook Event?

An Event on Facebook is just a Facebook page dedicated to a real-life event (such as a party), where you can send invitations and receive responses. On the Event page, you can list details, such as what the Event is for, where and when it's taking place, and much more.

Lots of people organize their events on Facebook, and these events may include birthday parties, concerts, anniversary celebrations, or just a small get-together at someone's house. An Event doesn't have to be large or significant. For example, you might like to create an Event for your book club meeting or to invite your friends to watch a play.

One of the main advantages to creating Events on Facebook is that most of your friends and family are probably already Facebook users, so it's a great place to grab everyone's attention and invite lots of people. You can send out invitations to all of your guests at once, and you can create an Event page where everyone can check Event details, RSVP, and coordinate with other attendees. Your invitees can let you know on the Event page whether they're able to attend, so you can check the Event page at any time and quickly see who can attend your Event and who can't. Let's get organizing!

ACTIVITY #35

In this activity, we're going to consider which types of gatherings would be suitable as Facebook Events. Think about the following gatherings and decide whether you would create any of them as Facebook Events.

* A birthday party for your grandchild that's attended by all of your family members

* A dentist's appointment attended by just you

* A dinner at your house with your two closest friends

Receiving an Invitation to an Event

If you've been invited to an Event, you'll receive an invitation! When this happens, a red number will appear on the notification button to indicate that you have a new notification.

1 Click the **notification button**.

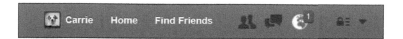

2 The notification will tell you which friend has invited you to their Event and the name of the Event, as shown here.

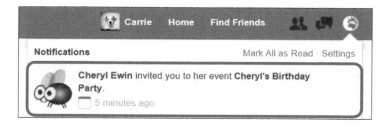

3 Click the notification, and the Event page will open. We'll go over the different elements in just a moment.

TAKING A CLOSER LOOK AT THE EVENT

From the Event page, you can find out important details, respond to your invitation, see who else is attending, and post messages and pictures.

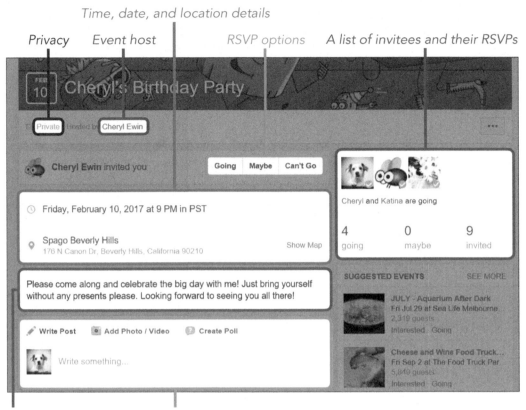

Privacy *Event host*

Time, date, and location details

RSVP options *A list of invitees and their RSVPs*

Event description *Post a message to the invitees.*

Privacy

The host of the Event can make the Event private or public. Private Events can only be seen by the invited guests, whereas public Events, including Event details, comments, and RSVPs, can be seen by any Facebook user.

Event Host

This section shows the name of the person hosting the Event. The host is usually the person who created the Event on Facebook.

Time, Date, and Location Details

This section shows the date, time, and location of the Event. If the host hasn't decided on these details yet, this area might be blank and will be added later. Don't worry, Facebook will notify you if Event details change.

RSVP Options

You can indicate whether you are going to attend the Event by clicking **Going** (if you're sure that you'll attend), **Maybe** (if you're not sure you'll be able to attend), or **Can't Go** (if you won't be attending).

A List of Invitees and Their RSVPs

In some cases, you might want to decide whether you're going to an Event (or definitely not going!) depending on who else will be there. This section shows the Profile pictures and names of some of the people who are attending. It also shows the number of people who have responded "going," responded "maybe," and been invited but not yet responded. Anyone who hasn't yet RSVP'd will be counted in the "invited" box. To see specifically who was invited, follow these steps:

1 Click the number in the "going" box, highlighted to the right, to view the names and profile pictures of people who have indicated they will be going to the Event.

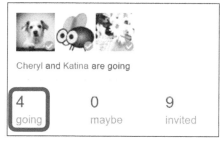

2 Click the "invited" number, highlighted to the right, to view the names and profile pictures of everyone else who has been invited to the Event.

3 Some people might not want to commit and will respond with a "maybe"; you can click this number, too, to see who has said they might go.

4 Click the X in the top-right corner of the box to close it and return to the Event.

Event Description

The host can add more details for the Event here, such as whether presents are expected, instructions for getting to the Event, the dress code, whether it's a surprise party, and anything else that's relevant.

Post a Message to the Invitees

Just like on your Profile and other pages on Facebook, you can leave posts on the Event page and comment on other posts. This is an excellent way to ask questions or add your thoughts about the Event, such as asking whether you should bring food or suggesting costumes.

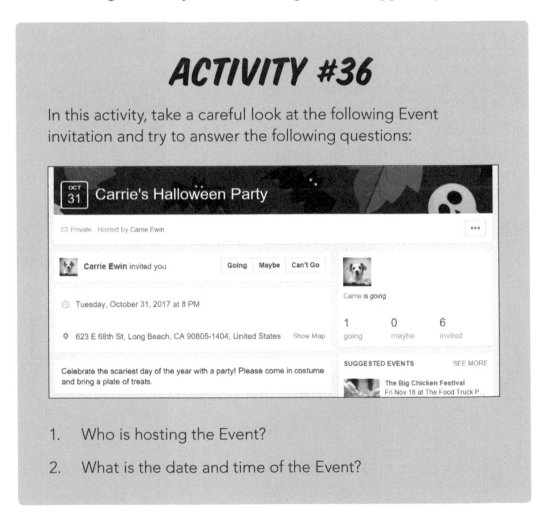

ACTIVITY #36

In this activity, take a careful look at the following Event invitation and try to answer the following questions:

1. Who is hosting the Event?

2. What is the date and time of the Event?

3. Where is the Event being held?

4. Are there instructions about the Event that you should know?

5. How many people have said they'll go to the Event so far?

RESPONDING TO THE INVITATION

Once you've been invited to an Event, you need to RSVP! You can respond by telling the host and other guests that you will be going, might be going, or can't go. The host and other invitees will be able to see your response.

1 Find the response bar under the Event banner.

2 Click once on your chosen response. You should make sure the response bar has changed to accurately reflect your response. It should now just show your response, rather than the three options, as you can see here.

3 If you want to change your response, just click your current response, and the other possible responses will appear in a drop-down list, as you can see next.

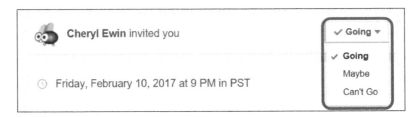

Be aware, though, that if your initial response was "can't go," you can't change your response like this. Instead, a button will appear that allows you to send a private message to the host explaining that you can now go, as shown below.

POSTING ON THE EVENT PAGE

Maybe you have some questions about the Event, such as whether anyone can offer you a ride. You might want to let the host and guests know why you can't make it to the Event, or maybe you just want to let everyone know how excited you are to attend! Fortunately, you can post comments to the Event page just as you can post on a friend's Profile page or your own. Everyone who has been invited to the Event will be able to see your post.

To post on the Event page, follow these steps:

1 Click in the **Post** box.

2 Type your message.

3 Be creative! Use all the techniques you learned in Lesson 5 to extend and improve your post, such as adding a feeling or location, tagging a friend, and including photos or videos.

4 When you're ready, click **Post**.

5 Your message will be posted and can be read by the host and all the guests.

REVIEWING THE INVITATION

As the Event approaches, it's always an excellent idea to review the details on the Event page. You may also want to check if any additional guests have confirmed that they'll be attending or have posted on the Event page. Here's how to open the Event page:

1 Open the News Feed page by clicking the **f** button.

2 Click the **Events** button in your Favorites section, highlighted here.

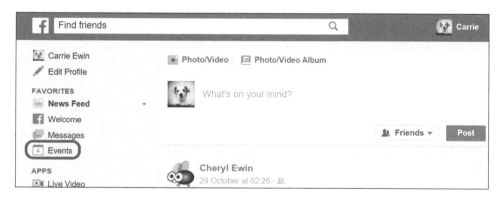

∗ NOTE: *If you created your Facebook account between 2015 and early 2016, and if you are using Facebook on Internet Explorer or Microsoft Edge, then your Side Menu may look a little different, and the Events button may appear in a slightly different spot.*

3 The Events Manager page will now open. This page can help you manage your Events. All of your Events will appear in the center of the page, like so.

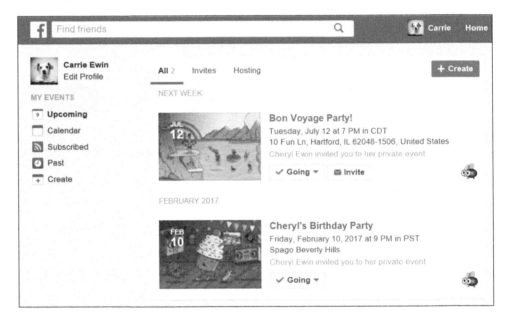

4 Click the title of the Event to open the Event page.

5 Recheck the details, such as the date, time, guests attending, and any instructions or comments on the Event page.

Creating Your Own Event

It's exciting to be invited to an Event, but it's even more fun to create your own! You'll need to create your Event first and then invite your guests.

To create your own Event, follow these steps:

1 Open the News Feed page by clicking the **f** button.

2 From the Events section on the Side Menu, click **Create Event**, highlighted next.

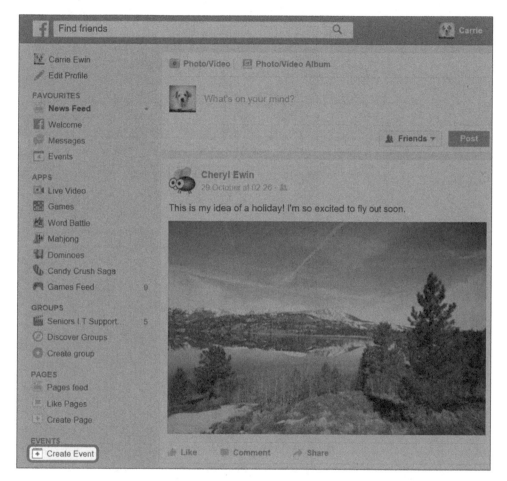

> **✱ NOTE:** *If your Side Menu looks different, you may need to find the Create section and then click **Event**.*

3 The Create Event form will appear. We'll look at each option on the form in more detail next.

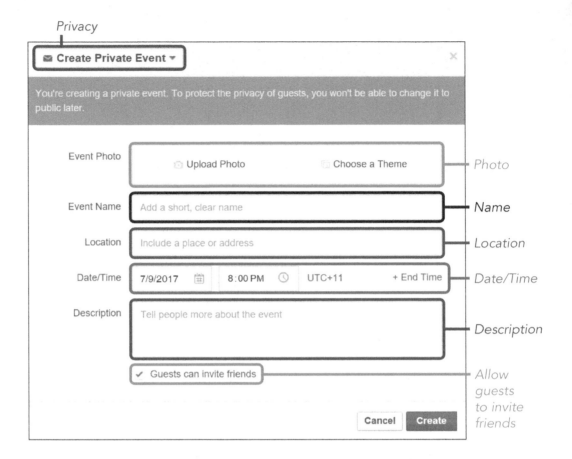

Privacy

Photo

Name

Location

Date/Time

Description

Allow guests to invite friends

EVENT PRIVACY

By default, an Event will be set to Private. A private Event can only be seen by the invited guests, whereas a public Event can be seen by every Facebook user. A private Event is appropriate in most cases; Events that are public on Facebook tend to be actual public events, such as charity concerts and street fairs. To change an Event to a public Event, click the **privacy button** to open the menu shown here and choose **Public Event**. (Think twice before you do this!)

EVENT PHOTO

The Event photo is the banner for your Event and will appear at the top of the Event page. You can choose to either add a photo from your own collection or pick a theme; picking a theme gives you a choice of a few stock Facebook images to use as your Event photo. The Event photo is displayed in landscape orientation, like your cover photo, so if you choose to use a photo, you may have to find one that fits in that long, rectangular strip. For this example, we'll use a theme.

1 Click **Choose a Theme**.

> Upload Photo   Choose a Theme

2 The theme options will appear. You can scroll with your mouse to see more images and themes.

3 You can also select a theme category from the top list to see more images, or click **More** to see more categories.

4 Find an image that matches your Event and click to add it as your Event photo!

EVENT NAME

It's a good idea to give your Event a clear name that summarizes its purpose because the name is the first thing your guests will see about your Event. To give your Event a name, click in the **Event Name** box and type the name. Be distinct and concise!

EVENT DETAILS

It's best to include the Event's location, time, and date when you create it so that your guests will have a better idea of whether or not they can come. However, if you're not sure where the Event will be held, you can leave the Location box blank and edit your invitation at a later date.

Add a Location

To add a location now, follow these steps:

1 Click in the **Location** box.

2 Type a location. If the location has a name, such as a restaurant or bar, type that name instead of the address.

3 As you type, you'll notice that Facebook tries to recognize the name and provide a matching location. If Facebook provides a correct suggestion, click the box with the suggestion. If not, then click **Just Use *your location***, shown below, and Facebook will accept the location you've typed—so make sure it's correct!

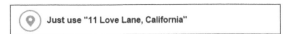

Set a Date and Time

Now you'll want to set a date and time for the Event. By default, Facebook will suggest today's date and a starting time of one hour in the future. Let's change it to the correct date and time:

1 Click the **calendar icon** next to the date.

2 A small calendar will appear, like the one shown to the right. Click the date of your Event in this calendar. If the Event isn't taking place this month, click the forward arrow to move forward through the months and then click the date of your Event.

◀		July 2017				▶
Sun	Mon	Tue	Wed	Thu	Fri	Sat
						1
2	3	4	5	6	7	8
9	10	11	12	13	14	15
16	17	18	19	20	21	22
23	24	25	26	27	28	29
30	31					

3 The date of your Event will then be set.

4 To choose the time, you need to type it in. First, click the hours section of the listed time. The hour's section will turn blue, and you can type in the hour your Event begins.

5 If your Event doesn't start on the hour, click the minutes section of the time and type in the minutes.

6 If you need to change the AM/PM section, click it and type in either **AM** or **PM**.

Add a Description

Next, you'll add your Event's description. This is your opportunity to explain the purpose of the Event and any important instructions, such as dress code, cost, and transportation arrangements. To add a description to your Event, click in the **Description** box and type a description.

Allow Guests to Invite Friends

At the bottom of the Create Event form, you'll notice a checkbox that allows guests to invite friends. By default, this box is checked. This means that your guests will be able to invite their Facebook friends to your Event. Depending on the Event, for privacy and space concerns, it may be a good idea to uncheck this option so that you have more control over who comes to the Event.

CREATING YOUR EVENT

Finally, it's time to create your Event!

1   When you're happy with the details you've entered, click **Create**.

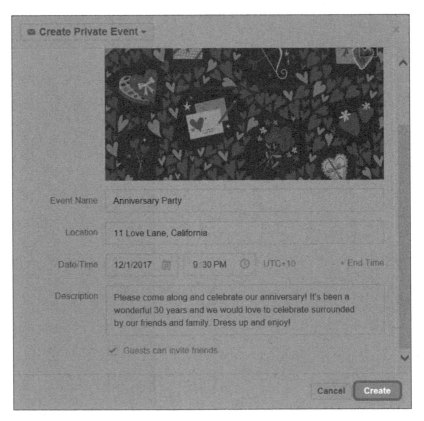

2 Congratulations, your Event has now been created! You'll be taken directly to your new Event page.

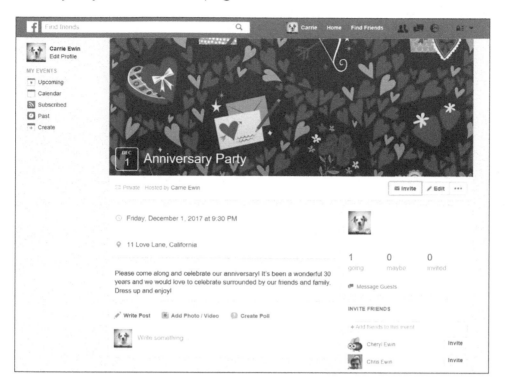

INVITING FRIENDS

Now you need to invite your Facebook friends to the Event! If you've moved away from the Event page, return to the News Feed page, click **Events** from the Side Menu to open the Event Manager, and click the title of the Event. Then follow these steps to invite friends to your Event:

1 From the Event page, click **Invite**.

2 Click **Invite Facebook Friends** from the drop-down menu.

3 The Invite box will then appear, which will list your Facebook friends.

4 A small circle appears beside each friend, as shown next. To invite a friend, you need to click the circle beside your desired guest.

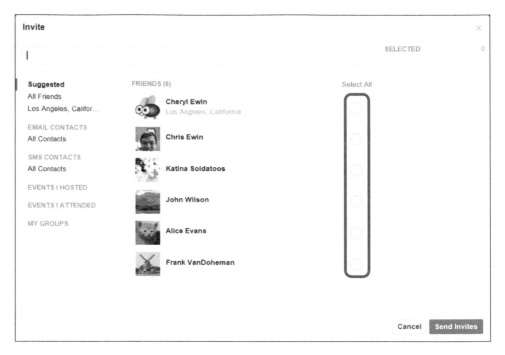

5 If you can't find a particular friend, try scrolling down the list or typing their name into the search bar at the top of the box.

6 After you click the circle next to a friend's name, it will change into a check mark. When everyone you want to invite is selected, click **Send Invites**, as shown on the next page.

7 Your Facebook friends will now receive an invitation to your Event. Wait for the responses to roll in!

ACTIVITY #37

In this activity, you're going to create an Event. Follow these steps:

1. Open the Create Event form.

2. Create an Event with the following details:

   * Event privacy: Private

   * Theme: Food and Drink

   (continued)

> * Name: Coffee Catch-Up
>
> * Location: Local café (choose a good one!)
>
> * Date and time: Sometime in the next month when you (and hopefully your friends) can make it
>
> * Description: "Let's catch up over a coffee."
>
> 3. Turn off the option for guests to invite friends.
>
> 4. Click the **Create** button.
>
> 5. Invite a few friends to attend your coffee catch-up.

RECEIVING RESPONSES AND POSTS

Now that you've sent your invitations out, you need to wait for responses. You might find that not all of your friends will respond right away, so don't worry if you don't get responses for a while.

When a friend does respond to your invitation or post on your Event page, you'll receive a notification, and you can use this to open the Event page and track your guests.

1 When a red number appears on the **notification button**, click it and read the notification.

2 Click the notification to return to the Event page.

3 From the Event page, you can see which guests have responded. Look just above the RSVP box and you'll see the names of the guests who've said they're attending.

4 If you have a lot of guests attending, not all of their names will fit in this space. Click the **Going** box to open a list of the guests who've said they'll attend, shown here.

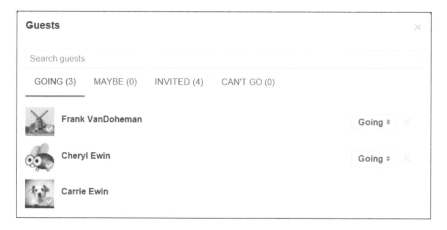

5 You can also click the categories at the top to see the guests who have responded with "maybe" or "can't go" or who have been invited but haven't yet responded.

6 Click the X in the top-right corner of the box to return to the Event page.

ACTIVITY #38

In this activity, you'll manage the responses to the Coffee Catch-Up Event you created in Activity #37. Follow these steps:

1. Keep a close eye on your notifications. When you receive a notification about your Coffee Catch-Up Event, open it.

2. Click the notification to open the Event page.

3. Have a look at the RSVPs to see who's going, who's undecided, and who isn't going. Also, check whether anyone has left any posts on the Event page.

EDITING OR DELETING AN EVENT

Sometimes something comes up and you have to cancel an Event or change its details, such as the time or location. You can edit or delete your Event at any time by following these steps:

1 Open the News Feed page and click **Events** from the Side Menu.

2 The Events Manager page will now open. Your Events will appear in the center of the page.

3 Find the Event and click **Edit** at the bottom.

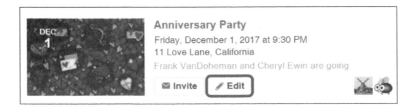

Anniversary Party
Friday, December 1, 2017 at 9:30 PM
11 Love Lane, California
Frank VanDoheman and Cheryl Ewin are going
✉ Invite   ✏ Edit

4 The Create Event form will appear.

5 If you would like to edit the Event (but not cancel it), use the form to edit the details and click **Save** at the bottom of the form.

6 If the Event has to be canceled, click **Cancel Event** at the bottom of the form, shown next.

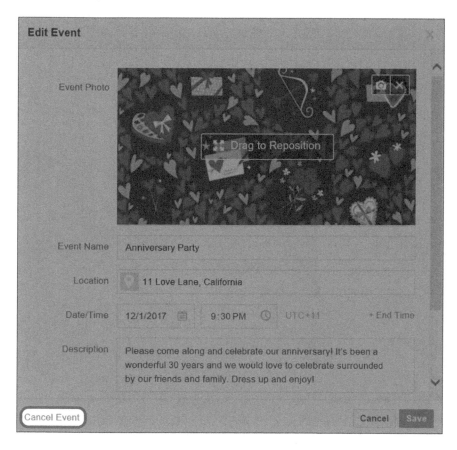

7 A box will appear asking if you would like to cancel or delete the Event, as shown on the next page. If you cancel the Event, guests will still be able to post on the Event page. If you delete the Event, the Event page will be gone for good. If you're sure that the Event won't be happening, it's best to delete the Event.

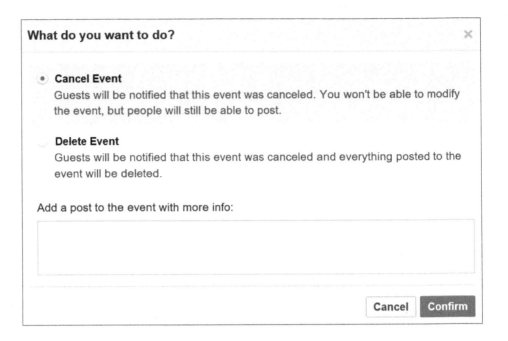

What do you want to do?   ✕

• **Cancel Event**
Guests will be notified that this event was canceled. You won't be able to modify the event, but people will still be able to post.

Delete Event
Guests will be notified that this event was canceled and everything posted to the event will be deleted.

Add a post to the event with more info:

Cancel   Confirm

8   Click the circle next to your preferred option.

9   Click **Confirm**. Your Event will now be either canceled or deleted and the guests will be notified (guests who indicated that they couldn't go won't be notified).

Phew, We Did It!

In this lesson, you learned how to respond to and create Events on Facebook. Events are a wonderful way to manage your social life using the huge network of family and friends on Facebook. In this lesson, you learned how to:

✱   Receive Event invitations

✱   Find important details on the Event page

✱   Respond to an Event invitation

✱   Post on the Event page

* Create your own Event

* Invite friends

* Receive responses and posts to your invitation

* Edit and delete an Event

Great job! Now it's time to fine-tune your privacy and security settings to make sure your account is safe and protected.

LESSON REVIEW

Congratulations, you've completed Lesson 11! Take this opportunity to review what you've learned by completing the following activities. If you can do so with confidence, then you are ready for Lesson 12. If not, don't lose heart—just keep practicing!

1. Create a new Event with the following details:

   * Theme: Food and Drink

   * Event name: Family Dinner at My House (or at a local restaurant if you'd prefer)

   * Location: Your address or the local restaurant's address

   * Date and time: Whenever suits you and your family

   * Description: "Let's eat and enjoy! Come along and catch up at a family dinner." Also, add details about the cost, dress code, and transportation, if any.

   (continued)

2. Turn off the option for guests to invite friends.

3. Click **Create** to create your Event.

4. Invite your family members to the dinner.

5. Post on the Event page that you're looking forward to seeing everyone.

6. Monitor the responses to your invitation so that you know who is coming.

7. Enjoy the event!

LESSON 12
PRIVACY AND SECURITY

In this lesson, we look at your privacy and security settings to ensure that your account is safe.

Why Is Privacy Important?

Facebook is a fantastic place to share information, stories, experiences, photos, and videos, but of course there are some things you don't want the world to know! Over recent years the privacy concerns of Facebook users have received a great deal of attention—and for good reason. The purpose of Facebook is to help you connect and share with others, but sometimes this might include sharing very personal information, such as the city you live in, when your birthday is, what your favorite hobbies are, what your grandchildren look like, and even when you're on vacation! Unfortunately, this information can be a goldmine to individuals and organizations that don't necessarily have your best interests at heart.

One key concern when providing personal details publicly is identity theft. Thieves can use the personal information you provide on Facebook to take out loans or even withdraw money in your name. A 2015 report revealed that in 2014, 2.6 million US residents over the age of 65 had been victims of identity theft within a one-year period, so it's well worth ensuring you are in control of your information.[1]

The details you add on Facebook could also be sold to companies and used by advertisers to pop up advertising material on the internet and on Facebook that is specially aimed at your age, gender, location, or interests. This can be invasive or annoying.

Of course, comments or photos you add to Facebook could hurt the feelings of others or even damage your reputation if they became public when you intended to keep them private.

If your privacy isn't secure, it's also possible that malicious individuals could break into your account. You could find that embarrassing or offensive posts have been made in your name, strange friends have been added, or requests for money have been made to your friends using your account.

1. U.S. Department of Justice, "Victims of Identity Theft, 2014," NCJ 248991 (September 2015), *http://www.bjs.gov/index.cfm?ty=pbdetail&iid=5408*.

Given these risks, it's important to ensure that your personal information is protected, and in many cases is only accessible to friends or family. It's also important to know what security risks surround Facebook, so you can make an informed decision about the type of information you share. In this lesson, you'll learn how to check your settings and tweak some important options to ensure that your information is safe and secure.

Viewing Your Public Profile

One great way to keep on top of your privacy settings is to check what other people can see on your Profile. It's especially important to be aware of what members of the general public can see. You may find that biographical information, interests, or even photos you'd prefer to keep private can be seen by the wider public. Fortunately, Facebook has a tool that shows you how your Profile appears to the public. This will help you identify any information or photos that should be better protected so you can take action!

1   Click the **privacy lock icon** on the Facebook Toolbar.

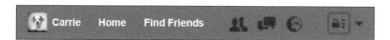

2   The Privacy Shortcuts menu appears. Click **Who can see my stuff?**.

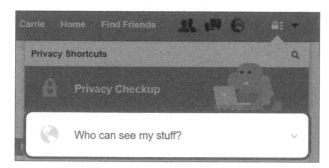

3   Find **What do other people see on my Timeline?** and click **View As**, as shown on the next page.

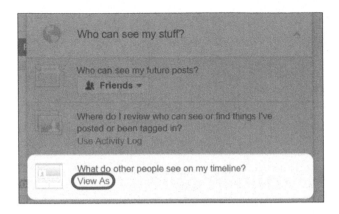

4   You might see a small tip window telling you about the tool. If so, click **OK**. If you don't want to see this tip every time, check the **Don't remind me again** box and click **OK**.

5   Your Profile will then appear on your screen just as it will to a member of the public.

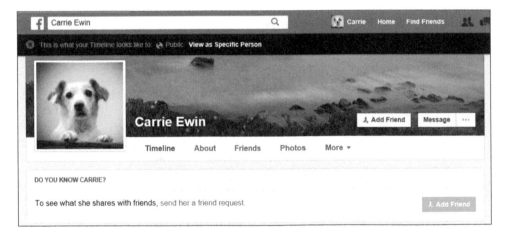

6   Look carefully to spot any information or photos you'd prefer not to share with such a wide audience. Don't forget to click **About**, **Friends**, and **Photos** to check these sections as well. (Remember, your name, Profile picture, and cover photo will always appear to everyone, as will any older Profile or cover pictures.)

This is an excellent opportunity to identify information you'd like to remove from the public's prying eye, but try not to be overzealous! It's useful to have some information available to the public to help real friends and family find you on Facebook. If you'd like to change the privacy settings for any of your biographical information, see "Editing and Changing the Privacy of Biographical Information" on page 59.

7   When you're finished viewing your Profile in this way, click the X on the black ribbon at the top of your Profile, as shown below.

8   Your Profile page will now reload and you can view and edit your information as normal.

ACTIVITY #39

In this activity, you'll check the privacy of your Profile by viewing it as a member of the public. Check if any of the following information is available that you'd prefer to keep more private:

* Written or photo posts

* Photos you've added to your Photos section

* Biographical information

Protecting Your Profile

After viewing your Profile as a member of the public, you may have discovered pieces of information that need to be kept more private. In this case, you'll want to change the privacy settings.

CHANGING THE PRIVACY OF ALL FUTURE POSTS

Your posts can include a huge amount of personal information, like what you're doing, who you're with, and what you enjoy, so it's important that these details (and any included photos) can only be seen by the right people. In other words, it's best for your posts to only be seen by your friends and not the wider public. To check who can see your posts and change this setting, follow these steps:

1   Click the **privacy lock icon** on the Facebook Toolbar.

2   The Privacy Shortcuts menu appears. Click **Who can see my stuff?**.

3   This menu will expand to show a range of options.

4   Find **Who can see my future posts?**, as shown on the next page. This option determines who can see any post you make on your Profile page in the future. This won't change older posts, only future posts.

5 Make sure this is set to **Friends**. This way, only your Facebook friends will be able to see any future posts you add to your Profile. If this option is not set to Friends, click the arrow, as shown below, and select **Friends** from the menu that appears.

6 Any posts you write on your Profile from now on will be visible only to your Facebook friends! When you create future posts, you'll still be able to change the privacy setting to Public or Only Me, but now the default privacy setting on each post will be Friends. Click the **privacy lock icon** to collapse the Privacy Shortcuts bar.

CHANGING THE PRIVACY OF AN OLDER POST

You can also change the privacy of older posts (and photos) either individually or for all older posts. Let's look at how to change the privacy of an individual post first.

1 Find the post you want to make more private.

2 Click the **privacy icon**.

3   A small menu will appear. Click **Friends** or **Only Me** to change the privacy setting of the post.

CHANGING THE PRIVACY OF ALL OLDER POSTS

Of course, if you would like to change the privacy setting of *all* of your past posts on your Profile page, you'll need a quicker way! Remember, though, you can't change the privacy of posts you've added to a friend's Profile page, and if you've tagged a person in your post, that friend will still be able to see it even after the change.

1   Click the **privacy lock icon** on the Facebook Toolbar.

2   The Privacy Shortcuts menu appears. Click **See More Settings** at the bottom of the menu.

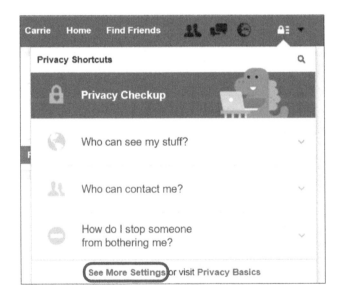

3   The Privacy Settings and Tools page will then load. In the "Who can see my stuff?" section, find the option "Limit the audience for posts you've shared with friends of friends or Public?" (highlighted next). Click **Limit Past Posts**.

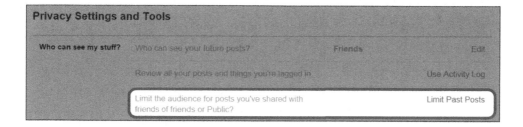

4   The following box will appear explaining that this will change the privacy of older posts to Friends. If you would like to know more about changing the privacy of older posts, click **Learn about changing old posts**. When you're ready, click **Limit Old Posts**.

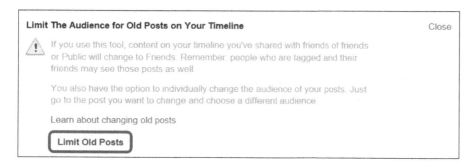

5   A box will appear asking you to confirm. Click **Confirm**.

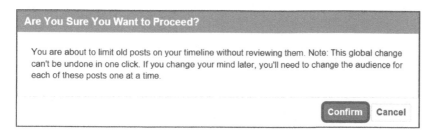

6   A final box will pop up to let you know that the privacy of your older posts has been changed. Click **Close**.

Controlling Who Can Contact You

Facebook is a social network that works best when other users can contact you and request your friendship. When someone requests your friendship, you always have the option of declining them! However, you may be uncomfortable with allowing strangers to ask for your friendship, in which case you can change your settings so that only friends of your friends can send you friendship requests. This will restrict your circle to a smaller number of people whom you are more likely to know in person and already trust. But be aware that this might prevent some family and friends from being able to connect with you.

To restrict who can contact you, follow these steps:

1   Click the **privacy lock icon** on the Facebook Toolbar.

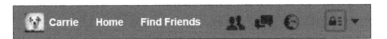

2   The Privacy Shortcuts menu appears. Click **Who can contact me?**.

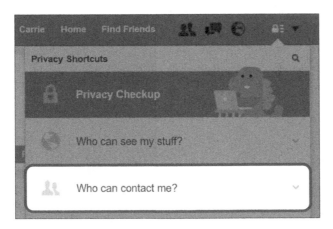

3   Find the "Who can send me friend requests?" setting, shown on the next page.

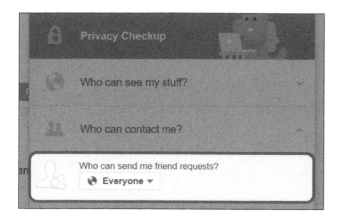

4   Currently this will be set to "Everyone," meaning any Facebook user can send you a friend request. To change it, click the arrow next to "Everyone" and choose **Friends of Friends**. Now only friends of your current Facebook friends will be able to send you friend requests.

Blocking a Facebook User

You may find that a particular person persistently bothers you on Facebook against your wishes by, for example, sending you lots of private messages, requesting your friendship multiple times, or inviting you to too many events you don't want to attend. This can be annoying and even scary if you worry that this person is trying to gather information about you for malicious reasons.

In Lesson 4, you learned how to unfriend someone, and this is usually an excellent first step if a user is bothering you. After your Facebook friendship has ended, the person won't be able to see your posts or any information that you limit to friends in your privacy settings. If someone continues to attempt to contact you even after you've unfriended them, you may need to block that person. Blocking someone means that they won't be able to see anything you post on your Profile (including posts with privacy set to Public), invite you to events or groups, send you private messages, begin a Chat conversation, or attempt to add you as a friend.

From any Facebook page, follow these steps to block another user:

1 Click the **privacy lock icon** on the Facebook Toolbar.

2 The Privacy Shortcuts menu appears. Click **How do I stop someone from bothering me?**.

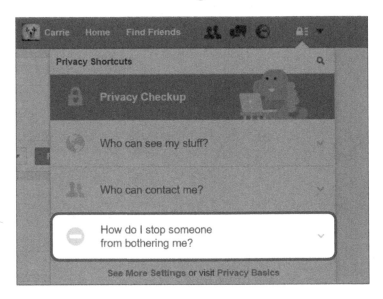

3 The blocking box will appear, as shown below.

4   Click in the **Add name or email** box.

5   Type in the name of the person that you would like to block. Be careful to spell their name correctly, and make sure to use the name that they use on Facebook.

6   Click **Block**, as shown below.

7   A list of Facebook users matching that name will appear, like so.

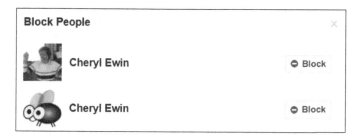

8   Identify the person you wish to block. You may need to use their name and Profile picture to determine the correct person. When you're sure it's the right person, click the **Block** button to the right of the name.

9   A confirmation box will appear asking if you're certain you would like to block the person. If you are, click **Block *Person's Name*** (for example, Block Cheryl), as shown on the next page.

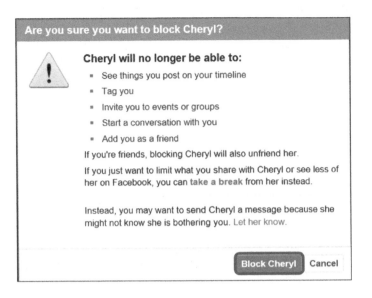

Are you sure you want to block Cheryl?

Cheryl will no longer be able to:

- See things you post on your timeline
- Tag you
- Invite you to events or groups
- Start a conversation with you
- Add you as a friend

If you're friends, blocking Cheryl will also unfriend her.

If you just want to limit what you share with Cheryl or see less of her on Facebook, you can take a break from her instead.

Instead, you may want to send Cheryl a message because she might not know she is bothering you. Let her know.

Block Cheryl | Cancel

10 The person will now be blocked from your account.

Choosing the Perfect Account Settings

A number of common settings, such as changing your name and password, are tucked away in the Settings page and are easy to miss. We'll look at how to change the most popular settings now to help you customize your Facebook experience.

REACHING THE SETTINGS PAGE

Almost all common settings can be changed from the Settings page. You can reach this page by following these steps:

1 Click the **downward-pointing arrow** on the Facebook Toolbar.

Carrie   Home   Find Friends

2 Click **Settings** from the menu that opens.

3 The General Account Settings page will appear.

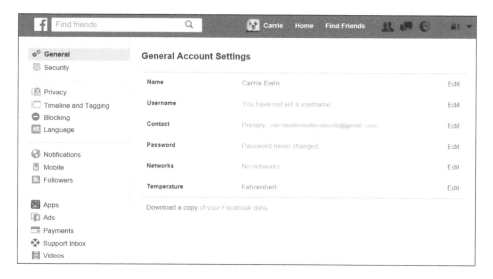

CHANGING YOUR NAME

You may want to change your name if, for example, you've recently gotten married or divorced or would prefer to be known by a nickname. Changing your name can also give you more control over who can find "the real you."

To change your name, follow these steps:

1 Click **Edit** to the right of "Name."

2 The Name box will appear.

3 Click in the **First**, **Middle**, or **Last** name box, delete what's there, and type in your new name.

4 Click **Review Change** at the bottom of the page.

5 A confirmation box will appear, asking if you're certain you would like to change your name and showing you options for how your new name can appear, as shown on the next page.

Preview Your New Name   ✕

Choose how your name will appear on your profile:

Carrie Ewin-Smith   ✓

Ewin-Smith Carrie

Please note: You won't be able to change your name within the next 60 days.
Learn more

If you're happy with the new name, please enter your password:

Password | |

Cancel **Save Changes**

---

6 Click the circle next to your preference to indicate how you would like your name to appear on your Profile.

7 To confirm the change, type your password in the **Password** box at the bottom and click **Save Changes**. Facebook will ask you for your password when you make a significant change like this, to verify that you are indeed the owner of the account making the change.

Your name will now be changed! You will not be able to change your name again for 60 days. Once you've saved the change, you should find yourself back at the General Account Settings page.

CHANGING YOUR PASSWORD

One of the best ways to protect your Facebook account from being accessed by anyone else is to change your password regularly.

To change your password, make sure you're on the General Account Settings page and follow these steps:

1 Find the Password row, as shown on the next page. Facebook shows when you last changed your password, so you can see if it's time to change it again.

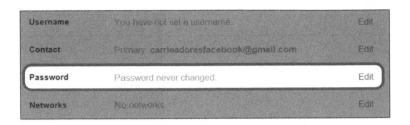

2 To change your password, click **Edit** from the Password row.

3 The Password box will appear.

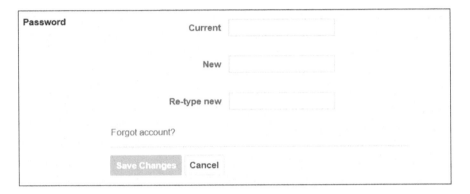

4 Click in the **Current** box and type in the password you're currently using. This is used to verify that you are indeed the owner of the account making this important change.

5 Click in the **New** box and type your new password. Your password must be at least six characters long and should include numbers, letters, and punctuation marks. Good passwords shouldn't be easy to guess and should be unique! If you've chosen a good password, the word "Strong" will appear underneath the New box.

6 Click in the **Re-type new** box and type your new password again, exactly as you typed it the first time.

7 Click **Save Changes**, as shown next.

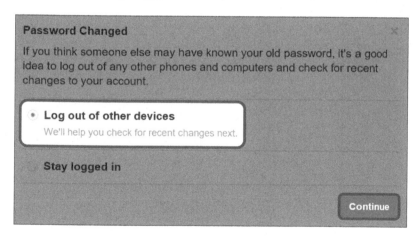

Password

	Current	●●●●●●●●
	New	●●●●●●●●
		Password strength: Strong
	Re-type new	●●●●●●●●
		Passwords match

Forgot account?

Save Changes   Cancel

8 A box may appear encouraging you to log out of Facebook on all of your devices (such as other computers, phones, or tablets). This ensures that your new password is needed to log in on every device.

9 Even if you don't think you're logged in to Facebook anywhere else, click the circle next to **Log out of other devices** and click **Continue**. This will help protect your account and make sure you're not accidentally logged in anywhere else (such as at the library).

Password Changed ✕

If you think someone else may have known your old password, it's a good idea to log out of any other phones and computers and check for recent changes to your account.

● **Log out of other devices**
We'll help you check for recent changes next.

Stay logged in

Continue

Your password has now been changed!

CHANGING EMAIL NOTIFICATIONS

Facebook likes to keep you notified of any activity you might be interested in, like new posts or replies on your Profile. You'll receive notifications on activity through the notification button, but Facebook will also email you about these notifications. This can be handy, but you might find that lots of Facebook emails quickly clog up your inbox! Fortunately, you can control the notifications you receive by following these steps:

1 Make sure you're on the General Account Settings page and then click **Notifications** from the menu on the left, as shown below.

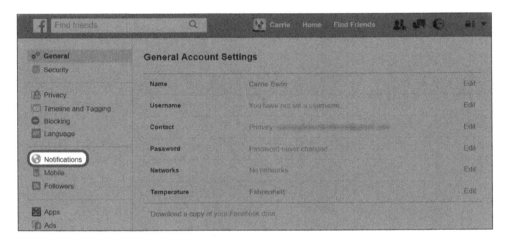

2 The Notifications Settings page will open. Find the Email notifications row and click **Edit**, highlighted here.

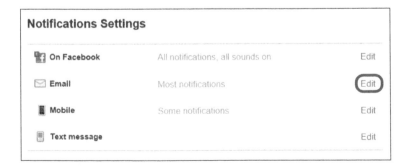

3 The Email section will expand, as shown in the following figure.

4 Click the circle next to the notification setting you'd like to choose:

* Choose **Important notifications about you or activity you've missed** to see occasional notifications about significant activity on Facebook.

* Choose **Only notifications about your account, security and privacy** to receive email notifications only about very serious Facebook activity. This is the option with the fewest emails sent to you.

Your notification setting will now change!

Securing Your Account

If you ever become concerned that your account has been hacked or that someone has accessed your account without permission, there are a few easy steps you can take to secure your account.

* **Change your password:** Follow the steps previously listed in this lesson to change your password. Choose a completely new password that you have never used for any other account online (such as your email or online banking account).

* **Log out of other devices:** After changing your password, you'll receive a confirmation box asking if you would like to log out of other devices. Make certain that you choose this option because it will log you out on every device and require your new password to log back in. This will ensure that the hacker is logged out of your account and won't be able to log back in.

* **Check your activity log:** Your activity log keeps track of everything you add to Facebook, like posts, comments, photos, events, games, Profile picture updates, and setting changes. You can check your activity log to see if there are any recent activities you don't recognize that might indicate that another person has done something on Facebook in your name. To access your activity log, follow these steps:

1   Click the **downward-pointing arrow** on the Toolbar.

2   Click **Activity Log**.

3   Your activity log will appear and you can read through it for any unexpected activity.

* **Report your account as hacked:** If you've done these things and you're still concerned that someone has access to your account, it's best to report it to Facebook. Facebook can help you regain control of your account. To report a hacked account, open your web browser, type **www.facebook.com/hacked** into the address bar, and follow the prompts.

Bidding Facebook Adieu

The day may come when you decide that Facebook isn't for you anymore. If you think you're ready to say good-bye to Facebook, you'll need to choose between deactivating your account and deleting your account.

While your account is deactivated, nobody will be able to search for you, see your Profile, or contact you in any way. However, deactivating your account isn't permanent. To reactivate your account, you just need to log back in to Facebook with the same email address and password, and everything will be restored.

Deleting your account is permanent and therefore more significant. You will not be able to use or recover your account again, and all the information stored in your account, such as your Profile, photos, and messages, will be deleted. Think carefully before deleting your account because you will never be able to retrieve it, and if you ever decide to return to Facebook, you'll need to build up a new account from scratch.

To deactivate your account, follow these steps:

1 Open the Settings page (see "Reaching the Settings Page" on page 270) and then click **Security** from the menu on the left.

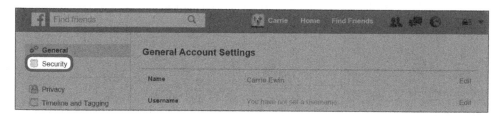

2 The Security page will open. Find the "Deactivate your account" row and click **Edit**.

3   The Deactivate Your Account box will expand, like in the following figure. Click **Deactivate your account**.

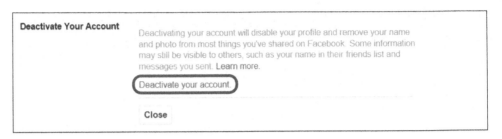

4   Facebook will ask you a few questions about why you want to deactivate your account. Follow the steps and click **Deactivate** to confirm your decision.

There is no option or button on Facebook to delete your account (they don't want you to leave!), so you'll have to do it another way.

1   Open your web browser and type **www.facebook.com/help/ delete_account** in the address bar. A box like the one shown next will appear.

2   Click **Delete my account** and follow the prompts to delete your account. Facebook will ask for your password and then will go through a series of security measures to make sure that the account is being deleted by you and not by a malicious virus, so you may have to answer some questions that seem silly.

The Help Center

As our last lesson draws to a close, you should now have an excellent understanding of the essentials of Facebook! We encourage you to continue to explore all that Facebook has to offer, and as you do you might find that you have new questions or need some extra help. Fortunately, help is still on hand! The Facebook Help Center provides a large array of answers to frequently asked questions on many different aspects of Facebook. To get to the Help Center, follow these steps:

1 Click the **downward-pointing arrow** on the Facebook Toolbar.

2 Click **Help**.

3 The Help Center will now load, as shown on the next page.

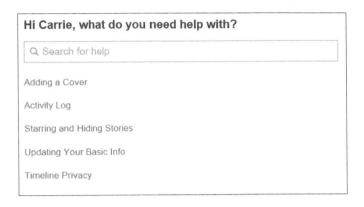

4   Type your question or the subject of your question (such as "logging out") into the Help Center search box. A series of more refined questions will appear, as shown next.

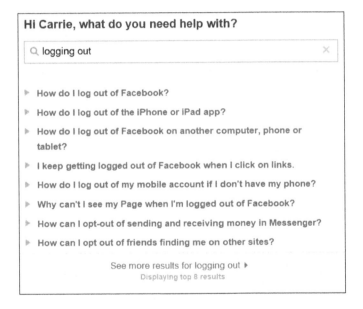

5   Click the question that best matches your own. An answer will appear!

6   Click the **downward-pointing arrow** in the Facebook Toolbar again to collapse the Help Center.

ACTIVITY #40

In this activity, you'll use the Help Center to answer a tricky hypothetical question.

On your Profile, you continue to see suggestions of "People You May Know." Let's suppose you don't know why you're seeing these suggestions and would like to remove them. Use the Help Center to solve this problem.

Phew, We Did It!

In this lesson you learned to use the privacy and security settings to help you stay safe and protect your information. Personalizing these settings is an excellent way to ensure that your information is only accessible to the people you want to see it. We examined how to:

* Control the privacy of information available on your Profile

* Control who can contact you

* Change your name and password to protect your privacy

* Control the email notifications you receive from Facebook

* Keep your account more secure and respond to an attempt from another person to access your account

* Deactivate or delete your Facebook account

* Use the Help Center

Thanks for reading this book. We hope you've enjoyed learning about Facebook as much as we enjoyed writing about it. But don't stop now— continue exploring Facebook and its wonderful features to find new things you love. Best of luck!

LESSON REVIEW

You've now completed Lesson 12 and this entire book! Take this opportunity to review what you've learned by completing the following activities. If you can do so with confidence, then congratulations, you're done! If not, don't lose heart—just keep practicing!

1. Change your password to a secure new password.

2. Think of any remaining questions you have about Facebook and use the Help Center to find solutions.

3. Click the **privacy lock icon** from the Facebook Toolbar and click **Privacy Checkup** to run a checkup. After you've completed each step of the checkup, click the **Next** button to move to the next step. In the three steps, make sure of the following:

    *   The default privacy setting of your posts is set to Friends.

    *   The privacy settings of each of your apps (for example, games) is set to Only Me.

    *   The privacy setting of each piece of information on your biography is just as you'd like it to be!

    Click **Finish Up** and then close your Privacy Checkup session.

SOLUTIONS

If you've gotten stumped by an activity, look no further—you're in the right place! These are the solutions to every activity in the book. If you're really stuck, most of the answers also include the page number where this information is discussed in more detail. If you find yourself flipping to the solutions frequently, don't lose heart—just keep practicing!

LESSON 2

Activity #1

To log in, type your email address and password into the boxes on the main Facebook page (page 22). To log out, click the downward-pointing arrow from the blue strip at the top of the page and click **Log out** (page 25).

Activity #2

1. The privacy lock (or question mark) button (page 30)
2. The Find Friends button (page 30)
3. The search box (page 29)

Lesson Review

1. Click your name from the Facebook Toolbar (page 29).
2. Use the Find Friends button from the Facebook Toolbar (page 30).
3. Use the Games button from the Side Menu (page 34).
4. Click the privacy lock button from the Facebook Toolbar (page 30).

LESSON 3

Activity #3

Click your name from the Facebook Toolbar. Your name and Profile picture will appear in the top-left corner of your Profile.

Activity #4

1. The Timeline (page 46)
2. The Intro box (if the privacy has been set to Public) or the About page on your Profile (page 46)
3. The navigation pane at the top of your Profile page (page 45)

Activity #5

Go back to page 51 for instructions on taking photos with your computer's camera.

Activity #6

Go back to page 57 for an example of adding biographical information to your Profile.

Lesson Review

Questions

1. At the very top of your Profile page in the navigation pane
2. In the Photos section of your Profile page
3. In the Timeline section

Tasks

1. To upload a picture you have saved on your computer, see page 48; to take a new picture, see page 51.
2. Go to your Profile and click the **Update Profile Picture** button on your Profile picture (page 48). In the Update Profile Picture window, scroll down until you get to the Profile pictures section and choose one of the photos listed there.

LESSON 4

Activity #7

1. Click in the **Name** box, type the name of the family member you want to find, and press ENTER.
2. Click in the **Hometown** box, type the name of your friend's town, and press ENTER.
3. Click in the **High School** box, type the name of the school that you and your friend attended, and press ENTER.
4. Check page 66 for guidance. You should find a Cheryl with a Profile picture of a cartoon fly and a cover photo of a cartoon sky.

Activity #8

1. Click **Find Friends**. Enter **Carrie Ewin** in the Name box, **Los Angeles** in the Current City box, and **Yale** in the College box, and then press ENTER.
2. Click Carrie's Profile picture to look at her Profile.
3. See page 72.

Activity #9

1. See page 66 to review how to find friends.
2. A red number will appear on the friendship notification button in the Toolbar (page 74).
3. From your friend's Profile page, click **Friends** and then click **Unfriend** (page 77).
4. Click their name from the search results list to open their Profile page. Click **Add Friend**.

Lesson Review

1. Anyone you want! There's no right or wrong answer here.
2. Click **Find Friends** and type your friend's name in the Name box (page 66).
3. Go to page 69 for help narrowing down your results.
4. Click your friend's Profile picture from the list to open their Profile (page 70).
5. Click **Add Friend** (page 72).
6. You'll see a red number appear in your Toolbar when your friend request has been accepted (page 74).

LESSON 5

Activity #10

1. From your Profile page, click in the **Post** box and type your message (page 83).
2. Click the **Post** button (page 84).

Activity #11

1. From your Profile page, click in the **Post** box and type your message (page 83).
2. Click the **tag icon**, type the name of the friend you want to tag, and click their name from the list that appears (page 86).
3. Click the **Post** button.

(continued)

Activity #12

1. From your Profile page, click in the **Post** box and type your message (page 83).
2. Click the **location icon**, type the location, and click it from the list that appears (page 91).
3. Click the **Post** button.

Activity #13

1. From your Profile page, click in the **Post** box and type your message (page 83).
2. Click the **privacy button** and click **Public** (page 94).
3. Click the **Post** button.

Lesson Review

1. From your Profile page, click in the **Post** box and type your message (page 83).
2. Click the **tag icon**, type the name of the friend you want to tag, and click their name from the list that appears (page 86).
3. Click the **feeling icon**, click **Feeling**, and choose a feeling (page 89).
4. Click the **location icon**, type the location, and click it from the list that appears (page 91).
5. Check whether the post is set to **Friends** or **Public**. Click the **privacy button** and choose the desired privacy setting.
6. Click **Post**.
7. You'll see a red number appear on the notification button when you have a notification.
8. Click the notification to see the comment, and then click in the **Write a reply...** box, type your reply, and press ENTER.

LESSON 6

Activity #14

Refer to page 108 for instructions.

Activity #15

1. Find the Post box. Click **Photo/Video** and then click **Upload Photos/Videos**. Find where your picture is saved, click the picture, and click **Open** (page 110).
2. Click in the **Say something about this photo...** box and type a description (page 112).
3. Don't change the default privacy setting.
4. Click the **Post** button (page 114).

Activity #16

Refer to page 116 for instructions.

Activity #17

1. Find the Post box. Click **Photo/Video** and click **Create Photo Album** (page 117).
2. Find the pictures on your computer, select them, and click **Open** (page 117).
3. Click in the **Untitled Album** box and type **Flowers**.
4. Click in the **Say something about this album...** box and type a description.
5. Click in the **Where were these taken?** box, type the location, and click the location from the list.
6. Click the **Pick a date** button and choose the date you want (page 120).
7. Click the **privacy button** and click **Friends** (page 121).
8. Click **Post** (page 122).

(continued)

Activity #18

1. Click **Photos**, click **Albums**, and then click the album you want to view (page 123).
2. Click the individual photos to see them in full size.
3. Click the **Profile button** from the Toolbar.

Activity #19

1. If a red number appears on the notification button in the Toolbar, you may have a new comment on your album! Click the **notification button** to check (page 127).
2. If there is a new comment on your album, click the notification to open and read it.

Lesson Review

1. Find the Post box on your Profile page. Click **Photo/Video**, click **Create Photo Album**, choose the photos you want to add, and click **Open** (page 117).
2. Click in the various boxes and enter these details (page 119).
3. Click **Add More Photos/Videos** and find more photos that you want to add to that same album (page 120).
4. Click **Post**.
5. Click **Photos** from the navigation buttons on your Profile, click **Albums**, and then click the name of the album. Click individual photos to see them in full size and then click the X to close them (page 123).
6. Click the **Profile button** from the Toolbar.
7. The notification button is the globe icon on your Toolbar. Check to see if there is a red number on the button.
8. Review Lesson 5 if you need help replying to comments.

LESSON 7

Activity #20

1. Click in the search box and type the name of the friend (page 132).
2. Identify your friend using their name, Profile picture, and any other information listed there, and click the correct result (page 132).
3. Complete the steps above using a different friend.

Activity #21

1. Click in the search box, type the name of your friend, and click their name from the list to open their Profile (page 132).
2. From your friend's Profile, click in the **Post** box and type your message (page 140).
3. Click **Post**.

Activity #22

1. Use the search box to search for a friend and go to their Profile (page 132).
2. Find the Post box. Click **Photo/Video** and then click the dashed square. Find a photo you want to post, click it, and click **Open**. Then click in the **Say something about this photo...** box and type a description (page 141).
3. Click **Post**.

(continued)

Activity #23

1. Click the **Profile button** from the Toolbar, and then scroll down your Timeline to find a post from a friend.
2. Click in the **Write a comment...** box and type your reply (page 145).
3. Click the **sticker icon** and choose a sticker to add to your reply (page 146).

Lesson Review

1. Click in the search box, type the name of your friend, and click their name from the list to open their Profile (page 132).
2. Scroll down your friend's Profile page until you find a post with a photo you like.
3. Click the **Like** button (page 136). Then click in the **Write a comment...** box and type your comment (page 137).
4. Find the Post box. Click **Photo/Video** and then click the dashed square. Find a photo you want to post, click it, and click **Open** (page 141).

LESSON 8

Activity #24

1. Click the **f** button to go to your News Feed and click **Games** from the Side Menu (page 158).
2. Click **Casual** from the list of categories (page 161). From the menu that appears, click **Trivia and Word Games**. Scroll through the page until you find WordCrack.

Activity #25

1. From your News Feed, click **Games** from the Side Menu (page 158).
2. Click in the game search box and type **Mahjong** (page 163).
3. Click **Mahjong** from the search results (page 164). When the page for the game appears, click the X in the top-right corner (page 165).

Activity #26

1. Click in the game search box and type **Mahjong** (page 163). Click **Mahjong** from the search results.
2. Click **Play Now** to set up Mahjong (page 169).
3. If you don't know how to play, read the instructions.
4. Try a few rounds of Mahjong!

Activity #27

1. Click the **f** button from the Toolbar.
2. Click **Mahjong** from the Side Menu.
3. When you're finished playing, click the **f** button.

Lesson Review

1. Click the **f** button to go to your News Feed and click **Games** from the Side Menu (page 158).
2. Click in the game search box and type **Solitaire Arena** (page 163), or use the categories (page 161). Click **Solitaire Arena** from the results.
3. Click **Play Now** (page 169), and play a game.
4. When prompted, click **Play** to play a tournament.
5. When you're finished playing, click the **f** button.
6. Find Solitaire Arena in the Side Menu. Click the cog to the left of Solitaire Arena and click **Remove App** (page 176).

LESSON 9

Activity #28

1. Click in the search box and type the subject of the Group you want to search for (page 190).
2. Groups will have the word "Group" beneath their name; to narrow your results, press ENTER on your keyboard and click **Groups** (page 191).
3. Find out more about the Group by reading the description (page 192).
4. Write down the Group name but don't try to join it just yet.

Activity #29

1. Click in the search box and type the name of the Group you found in Activity #28.
2. Click the Group name to open the Group and look at the description on the right side of the page (page 194).
3. The Group will say whether it is public, closed, or secret beneath the Group name at the top (page 194).
4. If you're not sure, do another search for the topic you are interested in and check out a few different Groups.

Activity #30

1. Scroll down until you find a post you like.
2. Click the **Like** button (page 201).

Lesson Review

1. Click in the search box and type **Seniors Love Facebook** (page 190).
2. When you see it in the list, click the Group name to open the page.

3. Click **Join Group** (page 196).
4. When you've been accepted to the Group, you'll receive a notification. To introduce yourself to the Group, go to the Group page and then click in the **Post** box and type your message; when you're happy with it, click **Post** (page 197).
5. Scroll through the Group page and read a few posts. When you find one you want to reply to, click **Write a comment...** to type your reply and press ENTER when you're ready to post it (page 200).
6. Remember that you can get to Groups from the News Feed by clicking the **Group** button from the Side Menu.

LESSON 10

Activity #31

1. Make sure you choose someone you are already friends with on Facebook.
2. Go to your News Feed and click **Messenger** from the Side Menu. Click the **New Message button**, type the name of the friend you want to send a message to in the To box, and click their name from the list (page 212).
3. Click in the **Type a message...** box, type your message, and click **Send** (page 213).

(continued)

Activity #32

1. Click the **New Message button**, type the name of the friend you want to send a message to in the To box, and click their name from the list (page 212).
2. Click in the **Type a message...** box, type your message, and then click **Send** (page 213).
3. Click the **sticker button** and choose a sticker; when you've found one you like, click it to send it (page 216). Or, to send a photo, click the **add files button**, find the photo you want to send, click it, and click **Open** (page 215).
4. Click the **Return to Facebook** button or click in the address bar of your browser and enter **www.facebook.com**.

Activity #33

1. You'll know you have a message when a red number appears on the message notification button in the Toolbar (page 217).
2. Click **Messenger** from the Side Menu and then click the message you want to reply to.
3. Click the **sticker button**, click in the search box, type **thanks**, and click a sticker to send it (page 216).

Activity #34

1. Look in the Chat List for any friends whose names have a green dot next to them (page 223).
2. Click the name of the friend you want to talk to (page 225).
3. Click in the **Type a message...** box and type your message (page 213). Use the **add files button** to send images and the **sticker button** to send stickers (page 216).
4. The Chat Box will pop back up automatically when you get a reply (page 226).
5. Click in the **Type a message...** box again to reply.

1. Click **Messenger** from the Side Menu (page 209) and click the **New Message button** (page 212).
2. Type the name of the friend you want to send a message to in the To box (page 212).
3. Click in the **Type a message...** box, type your message, and click **Send** (page 213).
4. Click the **sticker button**, find a sticker you like, and click it to send it (page 216).
5. If you've returned to Facebook, a red number will appear on the message notification button in the Toolbar when you get a reply. Open Messenger, find the reply, click in the **Type a message...** box, and type your reply (page 217).

LESSON 11

Activity #35

* Yes, all of your family members will need to hear the details, so a Facebook Event would be perfect.
* No, there is nobody else to invite and you won't need to share the details with anyone.
* Yes, even though only a couple of friends will be attending, you'll still need to let them both know the time and dinner details.

(continued)

Activity #36

1. Carrie Ewin
2. Tuesday, October 31, 2017 at 8 PM
3. 623 E 68th Street, Long Beach, California
4. To come in costume and bring a plate of treats
5. Only one so far, although six people have been invited

Activity #37

1. From the News Feed, find Events from the Side Menu and click **Create Event** (page 240).
2. Add the Event details; review the instructions that start on page 242 to see how to add each detail.
3. Click the **Guests can invite friends** checkbox to disable this option (page 246).
4. Click **Create** (page 246).
5. From your Event page, click **Invite**, click **Invite Facebook Friends**, and then click the circle beside the name of each Facebook friend you want to invite. When you're done, click **Send Invites**. See page 247.

Activity #38

1. When someone responds to your Event invitation, a red number will appear on the notification button in the Toolbar (page 250).
2. Click the **notification button** and click the notification itself to open the Event page.
3. You can see who is and is not attending in the RSVP box on the right (page 251). Posts will appear in the center of the Event page.

Lesson Review

1. From your News Feed, click **Create Event** from the Side Menu and then fill out the details; review the instructions that start on page 242 to see how to add each detail.
2. Click the **Guests can invite friends** checkbox to disable this option (page 246).
3. Click **Create** (page 246).
4. From your Event page, click **Invite**, click **Invite Facebook Friends**, and then click the circle beside the name of each Facebook friend you want to invite. When you're done, click **Send Invites**. See page 247.
5. From the Event page, click in the **Post** box and type your message; when you're happy with it, click **Post** (page 238).
6. Keep an eye on the notification button!
7. You know what to do!

LESSON 12

Activity #39

Click the **privacy lock icon** and click **Who can see my stuff?**. Find **What do other people see on my Timeline?** and click **View As** (page 259).

* Posts will be in the middle of your Profile.
* Click **Photos** from the navigation buttons to check.
* Check both the Intro box on your Profile page and your biography (click **About** from the navigation buttons).

(continued)

Activity #40

Click the **downward-pointing arrow** from the Toolbar and click **Help** (page 281). In the Help Center search box, type **people you may know**. Click the text **What is People You May Know?** and a small information box will open in that window.

Lesson Review

1. Click the **downward-pointing arrow** from the Toolbar and click **Settings** (page 270). Find the Password row and click **Edit**. Enter your current password and then enter your new password twice. Click **Save Changes**. See page 273.
2. Click the **downward-pointing arrow** from the Toolbar and click **Help** to get to the Help Center. Type any questions you have or a subject you want to know more about. See page 281.
3. Click the **privacy lock icon** and click **Privacy Checkup**. Follow the prompts to complete your Privacy Checkup. If any of these privacy settings are incorrect, click the privacy icon next to the information and click the correct privacy setting.

Index

CPSIA information can be obtained
at www.ICGtesting.com
Printed in the USA
BVOW05s1954051216

469845BV00001B/1/P

9 781593 277918